UNDERSTANDING AND TREATING THE PATHOLOGICAL GAMBLER

UNDERSTANDING AND TREATING THE PATHOLOGICAL GAMBLER

Robert Ladouceur, Caroline Sylvain, Claude Boutin and Celine Doucet

Université Laval, Quebec, Canada

JOHN WILEY & SONS, LTD

Other Wiley Editorial Offices

John Wiley & Sons Inc., 111 River Street, Hoboken, NJ 07030, USA

Jossey-Bass, 989 Market Street, San Francisco, CA 94103-1741, USA

Wiley-VCH Verlag GmbH, Boschstr. 12, D-69469 Weinheim, Germany

John Wiley & Sons Australia Ltd, 33 Park Road, Milton, Queensland 4064, Australia

John Wiley & Sons (Asia) Pte Ltd, 2 Clementi Loop #02-01, Jin Xing Distripark, Singapore 129809

John Wiley & Sons (Canada) Ltd, 22 Worcester Road, Etobicoke, Ontario M9W 1L1

Wiley also publishes its books in a variety of electronic formats. Some content that appears in print may not be available in electronic books.

British Library Cataloguing in Publication Data

A catalogue record for this book is available from the British Library

ISBN 0-470-84377-2 (cased)
ISBN 0-470-84378-0 (paper)

Typeset in 10/12pt Palatino by Saxon Graphics Ltd, Derby

This book is printed on acid-free paper responsibly manufactured from sustainable forestry, for which at least two trees are planted for each one used.

CONTENTS

ABOUT THE AUTHORS

Robert Ladouceur, Ph.D., is Professor of Psychology at Laval University in Quebec City. After his doctoral studies, he completed post-doctoral fellow at Temple University in Philadelphia. His work on gambling is internationally known. His model focuses on the cognitive variables in the acquisition and maintenance of gambling behavior. In 1996, he received a research award from the National Council on Problem Gambling, recognizing the high quality of his work.

Caroline Sylvain, holds a Ph.D. in psychology. Over the years she has presented many conferences and held workshops on the treatment of excessive gambling. Her doctoral thesis largely contributed towards the elaboration of the treatment development in this book. With her colleagues, she has developed a step-by-step treatment guide for excessive gamblers which is endorsed by Quebec Government.

Claude Boutin has published and reviewed many articles and book chapters about excessive gambling for which his expertise has received worldwide acknowledgement. As an active researcher and psychologist, he was directly implicated in the development and application of the treatment presented in this book. He also contributed to the step-by-step treatment guide mentioned above.

Celine Doucet is a clinician and psychologist who works in collaboration with the Center for Prevention and Treatment of Gambling in Montreal. As a researcher she conceived and participated in the treatment presented here. She also offers therapy for gamblers and their significant others. With her colleagues, she currently gives many training sessions about excessive gambling. She also contributed to the step-by-step treatment guide mentioned above.

1

INTRODUCTION: THE HISTORY AND PSYCHOLOGY OF GAMBLING

Although gambling has always existed, it has never before taken on as many forms as it does today. Let's be honest. Haven't we all, at one time or another, bet a few dollars in the hope of making an appreciable gain, or even an amount that would change our lives?

Gambling is an important part of all cultures, societies, and social classes. Nowadays, gambling is a common leisure activity and over two-thirds of adults engage in it on a regular basis. For most people, gambling is a relaxing activity with no negative consequences. However, others develop excessive behavior when it comes to gambling: gambling becomes a disease or addiction that manifests itself as an irrepressible impulse to wager money. For excessive or pathological gamblers, wagering is a source of both excitement and relaxation, which dominates their lives and has negative consequences. Among other things, this obsessive passion leads to the spending of ever-increasing sums of money.

Barely two decades ago, in North America, the Mecca of gambling glittered in the middle of the Nevada desert, magnified by the dazzling lights of Las Vegas. Day and night, 365 days a year, casino croupiers were at the service of any gamblers who leisurely took advantage of whatever moment was convenient for them to devote themselves to their favorite activity. In these luxurious casinos, where international stars often give their most recent shows, gamblers are still greeted with respect and deference. From the moment they walk into the casino, they are transformed, almost despite themselves, into princes for a day: they forget their daily grind. They live in a dream. They freely rove these gaming halls whose decorum rivals that of the most stunning castles of the world, and where the welcomes and smiles of the managers let them think, for a few brief moments, that they need not envy even the world's most powerful individuals.

If Las Vegas is still the Mecca of gambling, it must now share its previous monopoly with countless competitors from all over the globe. In fact, governments in most industrialized countries have discovered the monetary potential and gargantuan profits that can be drawn from gambling activities. Therefore, they have spread already existing games, and rapidly legalized and commercialized a panoply of new games. And they do this without hesitating since profits are virtually guaranteed, even before the new products reach the market.

Gambling through the ages

Modern society did not invent gambling. Far from it! With this regards, some facts found here and there in history document the perennial nature of games of chance through the ages,[1] even within societies that have been marked by intense intellectual and scientific development.

The Greeks

The Greeks, members of a noble and creative civilization, always gambled with money. In fact, the first traces of excessive gambling are found within ancient Greece, and at one time during that era gambling was prohibited in order to maintain social order. The presence of gambling during this era is revealed in the first volume of *Vie, doctrines, et sentences des philosophes illustres*. This first known historical document on Greek philosophy was written by Diogène Laërce, who probably lived in third century B.C. Even though Diogène was born at least 500 years after the events he describes, he nonetheless based his information on manuscripts, some of which have disappeared and date back to the time of Socrates and Plato. Although historians are often skeptical of Diogène Laërce, who is more often perceived as an amateur gossip than a methodic archivist, these critiques cannot undermine the veracity of the two following comments extracted from his work:

> *"Aristoxène, son of Spintare, says that he [Socrate] speculated, wagered money, won, quickly spent his win, and began to gamble again." Note that Aristoxène did not love or admire Socrates. In fact, he mocked him as often as possible."*

> *"It is said that Platon insulted a man who was playing dice. The other responded that he was losing his temper over a little thing, and Platon said to him: "But the habit of playing is not a little thing."*

Homer, the famous Greek mythical poet, reported in *The Iliad* how soldiers put their destiny into the hands of fate in order to choose the soldier that would engage in duel combat against Hector.

Thomas More's Utopia

Closer to our time, Thomas More (1478–1535) is probably the first well-known author to have proposed the complete eradication of gambling. In 1497, while a student, Thomas More developed a friendship with Erasmus (1469–1536). The latter, who was travelling by horse from Italy to England, passed the time by creating what was to become the best seller of the Renaissance: *L'éloge de la folie*. Published in 1511, this satirical text is written as a friendly letter that is personally addressed to Thomas More. Erasmus mocks the church and lawyers that are fiercely opposed to everything that is not optimally reasonable. According to Erasmus, the ideal society is one in which insanity poses no danger. In 1516, More responded to his friend by writing a socio-political novel, *Utopia*, which would later have its hour of glory. More reacted to Erasmus' ideas: He attempted to demonstrate that the ideal society could only exist by eradicating the irrational. For him, "Utopians" should never know dice, cards, or any other gambling game which, according to More, are all equally foolish and dangerous.

The Canadian Amerindians

The discovery of the Americas informs us about gambling, which was already common among Canadian Amerindians.[2] Jacques Cartier, the first explorer, related the existence of a custom among native women in Canada that scandalized him. Native women who were of age to wed, gathered to play games of chance, during which they lost everything. The playful activities of our native predecessors were subsequently observed by missionaries on a regular basis.

In reality, gambling has always been a part of First Nations' culture. In his exceptional book dealing with the history of lotteries, Michel Labrosse states that *"the refinement of these games and the intensity with which Amerindians engaged in them makes it plausible that they devoted themselves to these games a long time prior to the arrival of the French"* (p. 18).

What games did the Amerindians play? Mainly dice, drawing straws, and pick-up sticks. But, reprobation of gambling by religious and political authorities was quick to follow. Marc Lescarbot (1570–1642), a resident of Acadie between 1606 and 1607, was a lawyer, poet, and author of the first *History of New France*. He was outraged by the fact that some Amerindians were so preoccupied with these games. He relates that they spent a disproportionate amount of time on them and that some even wagered their wives! These extreme wagers were confirmed by a missionary who lived during the same period: brother Récollet Gabriel Sagard. In a narrative of his voyage to the country of Hurons (1623–1625), brother Sagard noted an abundance of these games:

> Gambling is so frequent and customary between them, that they devote much time to it. Sometimes men and women wager all they have and lose as gaily and patiently when luck is not with them, as when they lose nothing. I have seen some return to their villages, nude and singing, after having left everything behind. One time in particular, it happened that a Canadian lost his wife and children to a Frenchman by gambling; nonetheless, he voluntarily relinquished them afterwards. (p. 22)

In reading the works of Labrosse, signs of excessive gambling are evident within the first native communities. Games sometimes lasted three or four days, and ended only when a player had lost everything.

Gambling and worthy causes

Gambling has never solely been the subject of reprobation. As governments began to perceive gambling as a source of unlimited wealth, games of chance acquired a noble status. As France, Spain, and England disputed over New World territories, lotteries became widespread. Games of chance were perceived as an ingenious way of enriching the State while conducting useful and noble projects. Here are a few examples.

In the Netherlands, during the mid-sixteenth century, a ship-owner by the name of Jacques Henchoven organized a lottery under the patronage of the Duchess. Six hundred prizes were available, including a dish set, as well as silver cups and goblets. The Duchess, reports Michel Labrosse, advertised this event herself.

In England, Queen Elizabeth I (1533–1603) organized a lottery for the public good. Profits were used to renovate her kingdom's bridges and aqueducts. Also in England, Charles II (1630–1685) organized the first lottery whose profits financed American expeditions.

France was not far behind England and the Netherlands. Lotteries sprang up all over. Profits derived from organized lotteries were used to support charities and to help finance hospitals and churches. Between 1714 and 1729, over half of Paris's churches were restored with profits derived from lotteries. Lotteries became synonymous with altruism and magnanimity: Who would dare object to projects whose sole aim was the financial, physical, and spiritual well being of citizens?

Even large institutions of knowledge owe some of their genius to games of chance. In the United States, in order to enable the pursuit of the noble mission of scientific research and development of arts and literature, many universities, including Harvard, Yale, and Columbia, were partly financed by lotteries, or replenished their funds by organizing one.

In Canada, the origins of the first organized and officially recognized lottery is eloquent. Preparation for the Olympic games in Montreal, to be held in 1976, created a deficit that matched the grandeur of the projects of the city's mayor, Jean Drapeau. Given that games of chance were then illegal in Canada, mayor Drapeau found a clever way to bypass the law: he presented his lottery draw as a "voluntary tax" that citizens accepted to pay in order to absorb the deficit engendered by the Olympic games. In return, citizens were given a ticket, which allowed them to participate in a draw. Moreover, instead of giving a sum of money to the winners, they gave gold ingots!

The psychology of games of chance: why do we gamble?

It is important, first, to define clearly what we mean by "game of chance". A game of chance is characterized by the following three criteria: players wager money or an object of value, this bet is irreversible once placed, and, finally, the game's outcome relies on chance. This last criterion is central to these games and will be discussed extensively in the following chapters. Let us further clarify the term "chance". Chance announces and imposes the notion of impossibility of controlling the outcome of an event. Unpredictability is the key to understanding chance. Yet, gamblers do not always understand that the game is determined by chance.

The possibility of winning, however, is the *sine qua non* of all games of chance. Depending on the game, 2 to 50% of wagers go directly into the pockets of the organizers. This is clearly not the best investment that players can make! Why then do we gamble?

Research conducted in Canada and the United States offers some interesting and surprising explanations that are based on a thorough analysis of gambling itself. Ellen Langer, a psychologist at Harvard University, asserts that gamblers develop illusory perceptions of control regarding games of chance. When in gambling situations, players rely upon their abilities or skills, and develop strategies to beat the odds. Because of this, players overestimate their subjective probabilities of winning. Such is the case of Roulette players who spend entire evenings systematically jotting down all the numbers that come up, in order to use this information to place a winning bet at a time they consider opportune.

Henslin, an American sociologist, observed Las Vegas casino gamblers. He made a comical yet revealing observation about this illusion of control among gamblers. He noticed that "craps" players throwing the dice would modify the swiftness and force of their toss, depending on which numbers they hoped would result from it. If they wished to obtain a high number, they threw their dice swiftly and with force, whereas those who wished to obtain a low number threw it softly and slowly. Thus, the illusion of control reflected the amount of energy put into the wrist.

We have examined the impact of the role assumed by gamblers in our laboratories. We invited two groups of gamblers to participate in a Roulette session. The two groups were put into a situation identical to that of a real casino, with one exception: "active gamblers" from the first group threw the marble themselves, while the croupier threw the marble for gamblers in the second group (the "passive gamblers"). Whether the marble is tossed by the gambler or the croupier, the game's outcome is in no way changed, but results clearly revealed that players who threw the ball themselves placed much higher wagers and overestimated their chances of winning more than gamblers in the second group.

The most daily manifestation of illusion of control can be found in lotteries. Lotteries, by virtue of their availability and structure, are the most prevalent form of gambling in industrialized countries. Three types of lotteries are generally available to gamblers: "passive lotteries", where the number already appears on the ticket; "pseudo-active lotteries", where gamblers pick their own sequence of numbers; and "instant lotteries", for which gamblers find out whether they have won after they scratch a piece of paper.

By selecting the numbers they wish to appear on their ticket, pseudo-active lottery players obviously take a more active stance in the game. But, in addition to increasing their engagement to the game, they develop a greater illusion of control. However, from a strictly objective point of view, the fact that players pick their numbers in no way increases their odds of winning since each draw is independent from the preceding one.

Regarding this phenomenon, we conducted a study that was very revealing. We interviewed 200 "passive lottery players" and 200 "pseudo-active lottery players" after they bought their lottery tickets from lottery ticket vendors and kiosks. Among questions, we asked players if they would be willing to exchange their ticket with one that we had just purchased. If the player refused our offer, we then offered him or her three, five, or ten tickets in exchange for his or her one ticket. For pseudo-active lottery players, the ticket offered consisted of a number determined by chance. From an objective standpoint, the players should have exchanged their single ticket as soon as we offered two tickets. That, however, is not what happened. Pseudo-active lottery players demanded considerably more tickets than the other group; a large number refused ten tickets and some even said that they would not make the exchange for 100 tickets. Often, these gamblers choose their numbers very carefully to make up their lucky combination: one opted for a birth date to which he was faithful; another was using a series of numbers taken from a math manual of questionable origin.

As intelligent beings, we are not used to considering chance as an accurate explanation of events. We usually call upon chance when an event touches upon the limits of our competence, or when we encounter an extraordinary phenomenon. In fact, scientific research has shown that when we are asked to generate a random sequence of numbers, we are unable to do so. These studies demonstrate that people are generally incapable of producing completely random sequences and are greatly confused about the roles of chance and skill involved in different games. Research participants tend to avoid excessively repetitive numbers when they gamble, instead producing a large number of variations or alternations in the numbers they use.

We have noticed that this cognitive mistake is due to the fact that people are unable to take into account the independence of events. In our opinion, this stumbling block is the most important element for understanding the dynamics of gamblers, particularly excessive gamblers. When we ask gamblers to generate sequences of heads or tails, as in a coin toss, we observe that over 70% of people rely on past events to predict the next event. However, we know that each head or tail always has one out of two chances of appearing. Moreover, a detailed analysis indicated that the principal error is attempting to balance the number of heads or tails; they try to break all obvious patterns and avoid long sequences of the same event.

This same phenomenon was revealed by analyzing the sequences of numbers chosen by players of the Lotto 6/49. Despite the fact that players theoretically understand the concept of randomness, they do not use their knowledge of it when in a gambling situation and attempt to control the game by referring to past events.

What happens in gamblers' minds when they are gambling? How do they interpret this activity of daring to undertake, despite repeated losses, increasing financial risks? The numerous observations we have made in our studies lead us to believe that gamblers' cognitive activity is distorted; it biases reality and dupes its proprietor. Accordingly, it is essential to examine the individual's thought in a gambling situation. To do so, we used the "think aloud" method whereby gamblers are asked to express, aloud and intelligibly, everything that they say to themselves, including things that seem irrelevant. These verbalizations are recorded on a cassette and subsequently analyzed by the psychologist. The psychologist then classifies this rich cognitive material as either "rational and adequate" or "irrational and inadequate" according to whether or not the elements verbalized take chance into account as a factor that determines the game's outcome. Our first study employing the "think aloud" method involved slot machines, which are well known among casino gamblers. The results of this study were spectacular. Over 75% of gamblers' verbalizations were irrational, inadequate, or erroneous. In other words, the players' cognitions were not realistic, ignoring chance as the element that determined the game's outcome. Given the few subtleties of this particular game, 75% is a considerable percentage.

Our results have been replicated several times in studies conducted throughout the world among different types of gamblers and on various games. Furthermore, we have observed that the erroneous perceptions of gamblers are based on a common denominator: they commit the error of associating independent events with each other to predict the outcome of the game.

The different games of chance

Although we refer to them collectively as games of chance, one shouldn't believe that all games are equal with regards to their attractiveness to gamblers. We are just as much victims of our erroneous perception of the laws of chance as we are victims of the way the games are constructed. Theoretically or intuitively, we are well aware that we can neither control chance nor act upon it. Yet when we gamble, we act as though it were possible.

Certain games lead gamblers to believe that it is possible to have an influence over the game. For instance, when gamblers can decide when to stop the slot machine bar from spinning, they get the distinct impression that the result would have been completely different had they stopped the bar one second sooner or later. What a hoax! Similarly, having three winning numbers out of four on a lottery ticket, or obtaining three winning symbols out of four on a slot machine roll, can give gamblers the impression that they came close to winning. Gamblers interpret these "near wins" as fate's way of telling them that they should continue to play. Careful! The objective reality is completely different. In the machines that we use today, the outcomes of games are randomly programmed beforehand, so gamblers can in no way guess, predict, or modify the game's result. It entirely depends on chance.

Consequently, a game's potential to attract will vary according to certain characteristics. For instance, Bingo, Keno, and traditional lotteries, where the role of chance is more obvious, are less attractive. These games are probably less likely to foster excessive gambling habits than video lotteries that are suggestive of greater possibilities for control, which is completely illusory.

Blackjack provides another example of imaginary mastery over chance. Given that players are offered a choice between accepting and refusing an additional card, gamblers acquire the impression that they are the sole masters of their destiny. This game, which is always based on the random distribution of cards, obeys certain well-established rules that are collectively known as basic rules. Players must know that if the dealer turns over a card worth 7 to 10 points, he or she must accumulate cards until he or she reaches a score of 17 or more. If players are dealt two aces, they must automatically divide them to form two series, etc. These rules are in no way strategies, but are rather basic rules that must simply be applied when playing.

Similarly, informed gamblers may believe that systematically studying horse races will increase their chances of winning. In fact, studying a race track program will leave the neophyte perplexed and flabbergasted before the mass of information provided. The program indicates, for each horse, age, previous results, previous speeds at various points in the race, squad position, etc. Faced with such a quantity and complexity of information, gamblers must carefully study before betting. At least, that is what the horse race "experts" would say. But the reality is altogether different. Once again, chance is the only factor operating. Scientific research has in fact revealed that people who randomly bet on a horse obtain the same results as gamblers who call themselves experts and select their horses with care. What better example is there of deception?

In short, certain games attract players more than others, and consequently influence gambling habits. Among the factors that increase a game's attractiveness are the possibility of making choices, the speed at which the game is played, the apparent complexity of the game, and the number of "near wins" bet upon. Gamblers must learn to resist these attractive factors, or else dependence will track and take hold of them.

Gambling habits and excessive gambling

It has now been clearly established that the availability and accessibility of games of chance have an influence on the number of people who gamble. Unfortunately, when gambling is more accessible, more people gamble abusively and uncontrollably. In most societies where gambling has rapidly developed during the last decade, the percentage of excessive gamblers falls between 1 and 2%. The prevalence of gambling is clearly more elevated among adolescents. Gambling, like alcohol, can create dependence. The characteristics of habitual gamblers will be examined in detail within the following chapters, but let us take a moment to discuss some of the traits that are particular to this type of player.

Among other things, excessive gamblers believe in the methods they use while gambling. They are convinced that they possess the means and skills required to beat the odds. Sometimes gamblers win, and sometimes they lose. But even gamblers who win at first or over the short and medium term, begin to lose more and more often. Convinced that they are having a "bad streak", gamblers will start to wager money they cannot afford to lose. The money wagered on games of chance is essential to their daily life. It is used to pay their rent or mortgage, to ensure their family's subsistence, etc. Yet, they do not hesitate to wager. Are they not sure to win?

Any loss that gamblers experience is accompanied by an even more intense conviction that they are on the brink of winning. Gamblers who slip into a gambling addiction interpret their losses as a sign that the next bet will be favorable for them. After all, they ultimately say to themselves, "I can't always lose". From then on, gamblers no longer gamble for pleasure or to win, but rather because they feel obligated to gamble in order to recuperate their losses. They are swept into the spiral of addiction. Excessive gamblers or gamblers on the point of being so, become obsessed with gambling. They gamble more money than they anticipated, play longer than they planned, borrow or even steal money in order to continue gambling, etc. In short, gambling is no longer simply part of their lives: their lives are now at the mercy of gambling.

In this process, excessive gamblers generally go through three stages. The first, the winning stage, is linked to the gambler's first gambling experiences. Many gamblers remember having won important sums once or several times at the beginning of their "career". Generally, the amount wagered and sum of money spent on gambling is low, and they cash in their winnings, take advantage of this monetary surplus, and are even generous toward their family. No gambler seeks help during this phase. Even if gamblers begin to gamble more intensely, their behavior does not yet have negative consequences.

The losing stage is the second stage in the development of excessive gambling. During this phase, gamblers lose more often, but remain convinced that they can master the game and win again. More often than not, they attribute their losses to external factors and continue to gamble on a regular basis in order to chase their losses. Financial problems then become more apparent. Gamblers are then forced to borrow money and may even commit illegal acts in order to finance their gambling activities. At this stage, the gambling problem is already ingrained, but it is rare that gamblers will consult a specialist to help solve their problem. Only a small percentage of gamblers sense the danger and make the decision to confide their problem to a competent professional. In the eyes of the majority of gamblers at this stage, the consequences do not appear insurmountable, and most continue to believe that they can make ends meet by gambling.

Finally, the desperation phase occurs during which gamblers are still convinced that they will be able to recuperate money they have lost. But, after having lost everything, they experience many difficulties in the diverse spheres of their lives. Gamblers, frequently depressed, are at the end of their rope. It is most often at this last stage that gamblers undertake the first steps towards ceasing gambling activities.

Overview of the following chapters

This book traces a detailed portrait of excessive gamblers. The next chapter presents an overview of treatments that have been used over the last two decades to help gamblers. Unfortunately, these interventions have rarely been founded upon a systematic understanding of the psychology of gambling. Our knowledge about identifying these gamblers has increased considerably. By either observing specific behaviors or completing questionnaires, we were able to identify and describe several characteristics that allow one to provide a relatively sound judgement about the extent and seriousness of gambling habits. The following two chapters will discuss and illustrate the therapeutic means currently available to help excessive gamblers take control over their constant and irresistible need to gamble. These interventions are rooted in scientific research and evaluation of their results will give hope to gamblers who would like to put an end to their destructive gambling habits.

Finally, while ceasing gambling activities is the first goal of these gamblers, their second goal is the maintenance of long-term abstinence. Several strategies to prevent a lapse or relapse will be addressed in a specific chapter. Finally, we will share our clinical experience by describing the many difficulties we have encountered over the course of treatment for excessive gambling. We will also describe how we overcame these difficulties.

Notes

1. We thank Jean LeBlond, Ph.D. for having procured this interesting information about gambling among the Greeks, as well as for Thomas More's anecdote.
2. We draw some of this information from a book by Michel Labrosse, entitled "Les loteries ... de Jacques Cartier à nos jours", published by Stanké in 1985. Curious readers will find a limitless source of historical information on lotteries.

2

ETIOLOGY AND TREATMENT OF PROBLEM GAMBLING: THE DIFFERENT APPROACHES

This chapter reviews some of the different explanatory hypotheses about excessive gambling, as well as treatment avenues that have been explored. The theories on this subject will not be described in detail, but rather a general overview for informative and historical purposes will be provided in order to guide readers towards an understanding of problem gambling and its treatment.

A number of theories have been put forward to explain the development and maintenance of problem gambling. As of yet, however, there is no certainty about which theory or theories better represent reality. Nonetheless, awareness of these theories and previously experimented interventions contribute to a better definition of the context and therapeutic approach we have developed. Moreover, we will emphasize the cognitive and behavioral approaches, since they make up the framework of this book.

We have witnessed a veritable explosion of games of chance over the last few years and studies indicate that the more gambling games there are, the more people gamble. As a result of increasing accessibility, problem gambling is also on the rise and new types of gamblers are appearing on the scene. Presently, excessive gambling affects people with diverse psychological profiles and from all social classes. Unfortunately, in their search for support, these people will more often find themselves faced with an absence of resources, or with professionals who are inexperienced and unfamiliar with the problem.

Scientific interest in gambling is actually quite recent and has only begun to take shape over the past two decades. In fact, it was not until 1980 that pathological gambling was recognized as a psychological disorder by the American Psychiatric Association (APA). At that time, this professional association included a section describing the diagnostic criteria and the principal characteristics of pathological gambling in its diagnostic manual. Since then, despite the fact that knowledge about this disorder has grown, several questions still remain unanswered. It is obvious that excessive gambling has several roots and, accordingly, requires as many treatment options.

Increasing interest in the treatment of excessive gamblers led to the emergence of various causal hypotheses, each as interesting as the next. The most well established attribute the cause of excessive gambling to one of four factors: a biochemical disorder, an impulse disorder, an addictive disorder, or a particular personality structure.

Investigators first tried to understand why people gamble. They attempted to answer such general questions as: Why do we gamble? Why do we develop and maintain gambling habits? These researchers were also interested in factors that determine or predict the appearance of gambling problems. Various hypotheses about the causes of gambling problems were put forth, but the majority of them still remain to be scientifically proven. Despite increasing efforts, rigorously conducted studies are scarce, especially research on the prevention and treatment of this problem. Consequently, it is often difficult to draw valid conclusions about treatment effectiveness, since the results of these studies are sometimes unreliable. In fact, many factors can influence results if they are not properly delimited and controlled. Only a few studies on this topic allow one to draw sound conclusions.

At the clinical level, too few mental health professionals and resource people know enough about excessive gambling to offer a tailored treatment. Many professionals still address this problem as they would that of drug or alcohol dependence, referring to the similarities between these problems. However, excessive gambling has distinct characteristics, and those people interested should take them into account when treating excessive gamblers.

Therapeutic techniques are generally founded on explanatory theories and hypotheses, as indicated by documentation about the treatment of problem gambling. These works reveal that the conception one has of gambling problems (the development and persistence) influences the treatment approach used. The following pages provide an account of this relationship between theory and treatment, where the different explanatory theories of excessive gambling are briefly presented along with associated treatments that have already been tested.

Etiological hypotheses and the treatment of excessive gambling

Psychoanalytical theories

Psychoanalysts were among the first clinicians to put forth theories to explain the phenomenon of excessive gambling. For example, some proposed that an unconscious desire to lose takes control of excessive gamblers. Gamblers experience a strong feeling of guilt associated with unconscious hostility they feel towards authority figures, often parents, who imposed rules and restrictions on them during childhood. They unconsciously attempt to punish themselves by losing, which allows them to quell their impulses. From the psychoanalytical perspective, gambling is a forbidden activity that is charged with both pleasant and painful tension, and that provokes guilt and stimulates the need to inflict punishment on oneself.

During the 1980s, other specialists of the psychoanalytical approach attributed narcissistic personality traits to pathological gamblers. They described gamblers as people who believe they possess magical powers that provide them with control over the uncontrollable. In order to pacify themselves or to increase their self-worth, gamblers act as though they are quite dependent on external events and the people around them. Gamblers feel as though they are at the mercy of others and thus seek approval, which leads to experiencing strong emotional reactions such as anger and helplessness.

The "bad beat" theory, another conception of gambling that is based on the psychoanalytical approach, was proposed within the last decade. According to this theory, most gamblers have experienced several unhappy life events. These events, which are not linked to gambling and occurred long before the development of gambling habits, create a state of psychological vulnerability and foster the feeling that nothing goes well for them.

As an example, there is the case of a 30-year-old excessive gambler whose life drastically changed after a traumatic event that took place during his childhood. As a boy, he had always been the best student of his class until he changed schools in the middle of an academic year due to a move. During his first academic evaluation, his new teacher, who had not had enough time to estimate his abilities, gave him worse grades than he deserved. This unfair evaluation made the young student feel shame, accompanied by a loss of interest in school. Moreover, he never cleared up this situation which deeply affected him. These sentiments persisted into adulthood when he began making risky financial investments. Over the course of several years, he lost a great deal of money. These monetary losses, which he believed were unjustified, revived his feelings of shame and he attempted to recuperate his losses by gambling. Since then, he has been unable to break out of this vicious cycle.

This example illustrates what some people assume: that there are links between difficult or unacceptable past experiences on a person's psychology and behavior regarding gambling. These experiences serve as a springboard for other problems such as excessive gambling.

Adherents of this approach were among the first to study excessive gambling, which increased knowledge about its characteristics and manifestations. Unfortunately, most psychoanalytical theories concerning gambling are almost exclusively based on case studies and are difficult to verify. Nonetheless, these hypotheses are very interesting.

Towards the end of the 1950s, a few psychoanalysts attempted to help excessive gamblers. The psychoanalyst Bergler reports having treated approximately 60 cases and claims to have attained a success rate of 75%. However, no details are provided about the treatment conducted and its particularities.

A few years later, a group of clinicians offered group therapy for excessive gamblers and their spouses. This was another of the numerous psychoanalytical treatments described in the literature. Once again, the treatment components are not explicitly defined. Based on the idea that excessive gambling is related to marital problems, as well as other pathological interactions, the therapy aimed to resolve conflicts in their spousal relationships in order to eliminate gambling. For the first few sessions, group discussion revolved around the gambling problem and its consequences. At first, spouses perceived the problem as belonging exclusively to their husbands. They were unable to accept the idea that they may be playing a role in the persistence of the problem. But, after some time, a large number of them began to consider exploring this dimension. Then, as they progressively became more comfortable in the group, couples began to talk more and more about the conflicts in their marriages. The resource people were passive and attentive at first, and then they intervened and took on a more active role. In light of the conflicts expressed, and according to the discussions during therapy, the resource people encouraged comments and offered interpretations to stimulate reflections on how to resolve conflicts.

This group therapy allowed some gamblers to cease gambling entirely, and others to reduce it. However, there is no indication about whether these positive changes were maintained in the long run. Couples generally claimed that they were less anxious and less depressed, and that their attitudes were less critical following therapy. Couples also seemed to have developed more appropriate strategies for dealing with their gambling problem.

Adherents of the psychoanalytic approach recommend that people dealing with gamblers adopt an active, empathetic and reality-based attitude, which should make it easier to control problematic situations. According to the proposed hypothesis, gamblers who experience interpersonal conflicts can reduce their psychological vulnerability through therapy, which in turn may make them less susceptible to excessive gambling.

Among the few studies based on the psychoanalytical approach, many describe the experimental treatment too summarily. Unfortunately, under these conditions, it is difficult to verify the conclusions or to discuss them. Also, none of these studies seems to have dealt with important aspects of excessive gambling, such as the frequency of gambling and the desire to gamble. Consequently, it is not only difficult to evaluate their effectiveness, but their effectiveness is questionable.

Physiological theories

Physiological theories assert that a biological predisposition interacts with a person's psychosocial history and environmental factors, giving rise to a gambling problem. Towards the end of the 1980s, researchers observed functional deficits in the brain activity of excessive gamblers that are similar to those observed among hyperactive children. More specifically, these gamblers have a deficit with regards to inhibition, which results in difficulty controlling their behavior and resisting their impulses.

Around the same time, other researchers concluded that the impulsive tendencies that characterize excessive gamblers are related to a lack of serotonin. Serotonin is a biochemical substance that is synthesized by brain cells. Among its other functions, this substance acts like a neuro-mediator for the central nervous system and, according to researchers, is responsible for regulating impulsive behaviors. Studies that support this hypothesis reveal that excessive gamblers present common genetic characteristics, particularly regarding serotonin. However, no causal relation has been clearly established. Furthermore, knowledge concerning human genes still remains limited. Nonetheless, these studies are promising and warrant further research.

Other studies support the idea that physiological activation or the state of stimulation associated with gambling is one of the main factors involved in the maintenance of gambling problems. According to this hypothesis, some gamblers, specifically horse race amateurs, are deficient in the neuro-transmission of beta-endorphins. This is a natural substance produced by central nervous system cells and possesses analgesic properties. Low levels of beta-endorphins can result in a lack of stimulation. Gambling provides these people with an important source of stimulation and provokes a state of stimulation and excitement that compensates for the deficit. However, this does not explain why a person becomes dependent on gambling rather than on another activity.

More recent hypotheses propose the existence of a common physiological basis for addictive disorders and some impulse disorders (i.e., alcohol, cocaine, heroin, gambling, sex, food). This common basis is related to the brain's gratification system. This system corresponds to the dopamine circuit, which is a neurotransmitter that plays an important role in a person's pleasure sensations. If the dopamine circuit does not function properly, a disruption of the gratification system linked to pleasure may occur, thus predisposing some people to forms of dependence. Gambling, for example, temporarily stimulates the neurotransmission of dopamine, which decreases tension and creates a momentary sensation of pleasure and reward. Gamblers thus engage in gambling activities in order to re-experience these effects, but prolonged and frequent periods of gambling eventually produce extreme discomfort that can only be relieved by intensifying their gambling activities. It is as though temporary deprivation of dopamine increases tensions with the absence of stimulation of the gambling gratification system, which becomes the basis of the addiction.

During the last decade, countless theories have emerged that propose a link between physiological predisposition and gambling problems. These theories are extremely interesting. Many questions remain unanswered, but this area of research is relatively new. Non-physiological factors, such as social or cognitive factors, may also play a role in the development and persistence of problem gambling. These factors merit special consideration, and theories that integrate such factors are presented in the following sections.

Treatment based on physiological theories obviously led to the development of treatments. Based on the assumption that excessive gambling has a physiological cause and is similar to a disease, researchers attempted to treat the problem with medication. Clinical trials involving these drugs are currently in full bloom. Pharmacological trials allow for the evaluation of different types of medication all over the world. Among the medications administered in recent years, lithium has been used to reduce impulsiveness and gambling behavior. Some researchers have also administered antidepressants to gamblers, particularly a kind that is generally used to decrease obsessive and compulsive behavior since gambling is often considered as such. Finally, other studies have assessed drugs that have been proven effective for people who are dependent on alcohol. The result sought through use of this medication is the elimination of the euphoric effects that often accompany gambling. Thus, as a gambler's need to gamble loses its intensity, the desire to gamble decreases. The same medication is also used to reduce the risk of relapse.

These various drugs are assumed to have beneficial therapeutic effects for excessive gamblers. Generally speaking, several medications have produced positive results, while others have produced less interesting results; some have even had serious side effects. Moreover, as most pharmacotherapeutic experiments conducted so far have involved only a small number of gamblers, there is still a lack of information about the effects of these treatments on a greater number of individuals. These pharmacological studies regarding the treatment of gambling are therefore exploratory. While some results are promising, more studies are needed to confirm the effectiveness of previously tested medication or to find new ones that might have even better effects. Studies such as these would allow the prescription of medication on a larger scale.

According to researchers who evaluate the effectiveness of these drugs, none is considered to possess magical powers. Even if some medications seem to be effective and physically well tolerated, these researchers recommend rather that they be used in conjunction with cognitive and behavioral treatments, or other non-pharmacological therapies or activities such as participation in support groups, consultation of a personal financial planner, etc.

Behavioral theories

Since the end of the 1960s, behaviorists have put forward various hypotheses to explain excessive gambling. Contrary to psychoanalytical and physiological approaches, which propose, respectively, that the cause of excessive gambling is linked to childhood trauma or a physiological malfunction, the behavioral approach views it rather as a behavioral disorder. It also differs from the psychoanalytical and physiological approaches by its method of assessment, observation, as well as treatment. For example, this theory supports the idea that excessive gambling is a learned behavior. More specifically, monetary or financial gain has been the focus of several explanatory hypotheses. It has been proposed that occasional monetary gains have an intermittently reinforcing effect, which favors the persistence to gamble. For others, winning an important sum of money during early gambling experiences, a period that often determines the development of gambling habits, creates a predisposition to gamble excessively. In fact, first wins often stimulate interest in gambling among many gamblers.

Monetary gains were still considered to be an important reinforcer during the 1980s, but other elements were integrated into the hypotheses formulated by researchers. Some hypothesized that, in addition to monetary gain, another type of reinforcer contributes to the development and maintenance of gambling: excitement and stimulation. According to this perspective, the excitement a gambler experiences is the result of many different events that occur throughout the gambling session and is associated with physiological activation.

Other researchers assert that the development of diverse behaviors, such as gambling, is learned by observing others. For instance, some individuals are initiated to gambling in the company of family members. Our own clinical experience reveals that a large number of excessive gamblers report having been repeatedly exposed to gambling during their childhood and that their parents gambled regularly. Some parents displayed behaviors and held attitudes that could lead one to believe that they too had a gambling problem. Given that such behaviors are familiar to them, children are susceptible to imitating these same behaviors since they have not been warned about the consequences of gambling.

Behavioral hypotheses provide interesting leads for better understanding how gambling habits and problems may appear and develop. However, other factors also seem to play a role. The cognitive dimension, as well as the combination of cognitive and behavioral dimensions, allow for a more comprehensive explanation of the issue. These new elements will be discussed later.

Over the last few decades, a number of treatments aimed at modifying gambling behavior have been proposed and tested. These treatments have solidly backed up the development of new types of interventions. Let us examine some behavioral treatments that are offered nowadays and are described in gambling literature.

Until now, most existing treatments for excessive gambling are rooted in the behavioral model and have generally been found to be effective. However, many of the studies combined various behavioral techniques, complicating the assessment of the effectiveness of each. In spite of this, much effort has been invested into the development of behavior modification treatments, and although some of these are considered inappropriate by current standards, they acted as a springboard for the development of new treatments.

Behavioral therapies became very popular during the 1960s. Within the behavioral perspective, "aversive conditioning" was frequently applied. Generally, these therapies aimed to reduce the frequency of an undesirable behavior by associating it with an unpleasant stimulus or condition. In order to modify gamblers' behavior, some therapies resorted to an aversive method using electric shocks to eliminate the gamblers' desire to gamble.

Nowadays, nobody would dare do such a thing. At the time, however, a small portable appliance was attached to gamblers' left wrists. Then, after having recreated the atmosphere of a gaming parlor, gamblers were simply placed in a simulated gambling situation. While they engaged in their favorite activity, gamblers received an aversive stimulation, at 30- to 120-second intervals throughout the entire gambling session. This way of doing things seems shocking and almost implausible today but, at the time, researchers strongly believed in the effectiveness of aversive therapies.

In another treatment, gamblers were subjected to one of two conditions. Every 15 seconds over the course of a gambling session, they would either receive an electric shock or hear an alarm. Gamblers could never predict which of the two events would occur. This inability to predict would, according to investigators, provoke anxiety and consequently result in a progressive loss of interest in gambling. Finally, in another experiment, gamblers were asked to flip through the pages of a newspaper that contained information about gambling, specifically about horse racing. Although the gamblers knew this information was there, they did not know the pages on which this information could be found. When they came across a page that contained information about gambling, they received an aversive stimulation. Over the course of treatment, their interest in gambling decreased.

It is difficult to imagine that these treatments were used less than 30 years ago, but they correspond to the theoretical model of that time and it goes without saying that these types of therapies no longer exist. Although positive results had been obtained for some gamblers, it was certainly not the case for all those who were treated in that period. These treatments now seem to be completely inappropriate and unacceptable and, as we will see later, present-day treatments have been enormously refined.

Other treatment methods based on the behavioral model have replaced aversive therapy and have been tested over the last two decades. For instance, some therapists treated gamblers with stimulus control or exposure to gambling. In the treatment based on stimulus control, therapists provide concrete suggestions to gamblers on how to control their gambling behavior. For instance, gamblers may be told to avoid risky routes or roads that lead to gambling establishments, to give their paycheck to a trusted third person, and to carry only small sums of money. In the treatment based on exposure to gambling, the resource person accompanies gamblers to gambling establishments and progressively distance themselves if gamblers manage without giving in to their urge to gamble. Positive results have been reported for this treatment among a small number of gamblers.

A treatment based on a procedure called imaginal desensitization has also been developed. This procedure generally involves describing to a person a scenario that involves a problematic behavior, while associating it with a period of relaxation. Once relaxed, the person must first imagine acting as the scenario presented by the speaker suggests. Generally, just imagining the scenario leads to some excitement or intense stimulation. Then, once relaxed, the person must imagine a second problematic behavior and repeat the same process.

Imaginal desensitization aims to reduce gamblers' compulsive behavior by decreasing the degree of excitement or stimulation they experience when gambling. Scenarios, which inevitably stimulate the urge to gamble, are described to the gambler being treated. The gambler then receives brief relaxation training that involves contracting and relaxing his or her muscles. The gambler is then asked to imagine the first scene, then indicate when he or she feels relaxed again. After 20 seconds of relaxation, the gambler must imagine the second scenario in which he or she leaves the gambling situation. After one minute, the second scenario is presented to the gambler, and so on. The scenarios are thus successively presented over a period of 15 minutes.

A similar treatment based on imaginal relaxation was tested during the same period. In this case, gamblers are trained to relax and are then asked to create relaxing images in their minds. The goal of this intervention is to attain better mastery over their tensions; assuming that gamblers become better prepared to react calmly to situations that are related to gambling or might stimulate and excite them.

One study that compared imaginal desensitization therapy to imaginal relaxation therapy, showed that the two treatments were equally effective. Another study – comparing the results of imaginal desensitization, aversive therapy, imaginal relaxation, and exposure therapy – indicated that imaginal desensitization is slightly more effective than the other three techniques.

Cognitive theory

Behavioral treatment of excessive gambling allowed for the exploration of many new intervention possibilities. However, other aspects of gambling warrant description, such as cognitive factors, which also seem to play a role in the appearance of these problems. In fact, since the beginning of the 1990s, the cognitive approach has increased in popularity, while the cognitive processes have captured, more and more, the attention of investigators in the field of excessive gambling.

Essentially, specialists of this approach are interested in the way that individuals perceive their reality and problems. They work towards modifying thoughts that lead to difficulties. In the case of excessive gambling, they determine gamblers' perceptions of gambling and make them aware that some of their thoughts or interpretations are erroneous and harmful. Cognitive therapy is therefore aimed at correcting thoughts that foster the gambler's urge to gamble. This therapeutic approach is described in detail in Chapter 5, which deals with the treatment of excessive gambling.

Adherents of the cognitive approach assert that gamblers fail to take into account the negative winning expectancy involved in games of chance. This aspect appears to be a determinant of regular participation in gambling games, and the persistence of gambling habits. Negative winning expectancy, which is a characteristic element of all games of chance, means that it is impossible for a gambler to make gains by gambling in the long run. These games serve to enrich their organizers above all, and they are conceived in such a way that they invariably put gamblers at an unfair disadvantage – particularly those who gamble regularly. Excessive gamblers persist in gambling because they believe that the outcome of the game will be in their favor. Actually, when in a gambling context, gamblers entertain a series of false or erroneous beliefs or perceptions that are at the very core of their persistence to gamble.

Our own studies on the subject have in fact allowed us to conclude that these erroneous perceptions are at the basis of the development and maintenance of gambling problems. They are also strongly related to an increase in the frequency of gambling as well as an increase in bets. These erroneous cognitions lead gamblers to think that they can control the game and predict the result. Gamblers try to understand the "system" and seek strategies that will allow them to beat it. However, what they do not know, or do not take into account, is that they have absolutely no control or ability to predict anything at all, since it is chance alone that determines the outcome of these games. Gamblers have no power over the course of the game, and even by relying on years of observation, it is completely impossible to improve their way of playing. In reality, the observation of gambling events is not only useless, but often counter-productive since it gives rise to and maintains erroneous beliefs.

Excessive gamblers believe there are strategies that will help them to win and seek foolproof recipes, without doubting that they do not exist. Furthermore, when they win, they attribute their wins to their skills, believing they have found the "right way to play". Many gamblers firmly believe that a win results from an accurate prediction or their power over the game. On the other hand, they place little value on their unsuccessful turns and generally attribute them to circumstances beyond their control.

This phenomenon, whereby gamblers make a causal link between their actions and the result of a game, is commonly called the illusion of control, and rare are the gamblers who do not fall into this trap. This illusion of control touches upon the majority of gamblers, with variable intensity. Several factors, such as competition, voluntary engagement, active participation, familiarity of practice, have effects on the intensity of the illusion of control. Moreover, behaviors marked by superstition are very frequently associated with this phenomenon. Gamblers thus carry out certain gestures that have no apparent link with the game, such as wearing certain clothing or having a lucky object. Furthermore, gamblers poorly evaluate the probabilities of winning and are persuaded that they will inevitably win one day. For the most part, their erroneous belief that an important win is imminent ensures that they continue gambling. However, according to the law of probabilities, those who play games of chance have slim chances of making a substantial gain.

Tenants of the cognitive approach therefore feel that cognitive factors are essential to understanding the persistence to gamble. Cognitive errors, in a gambling context, can be observed among both occasional and excessive gamblers, which means that the reason some people gamble moderately and others excessively cannot be explained. Nobody doubts that the combination of erroneous perceptions with other factors more accurately explains the acquisition and persistence of gambling problems.

Regarding treatment, therapy exploiting the cognitive approach is based on a model that puts a person's emotions in relation to his or her behaviors and thoughts. People who consult specialists for psychological difficulties do not always understand the basis of their problem and its associated elements. In this sense, cognitive therapy proposes a new understanding of their problem. The data obtained and experiences over the course of therapy are taken advantage of and become preferred intervention targets.

Cognitive therapy is of short duration. It lasts only 10 to 15 meetings. This brevity favors autonomy and decreases the risk of dependence. Furthermore, gamblers are invited to take advantage of each moment and, actively, to participate as much as possible. Within this framework, collaboration is crucial and meetings are concerned with the present. The therapy is concerned with the gambler's experiences over the course of therapy, rather than seeking the problem's deep causes and analyzing traumatic events in childhood in detail, as would a specialist of the psychoanalytical approach. The resource person conducting cognitive therapy is more interested in the thoughts and events that occur in daily life that are related, closely or otherwise, to the desire to gamble. By focusing on their method of learning in their current experience, gamblers are better equipped to face similar situations in the future.

In cognitive therapy, both gamblers and resource people are perceived as experts: gamblers know their difficulties well, while the therapists provide a rational order to them and cognitive strategies to overcome them. Gamblers are thus called upon to participate actively in treatment and seek solutions in collaboration with their resource person. The structure, which is the same throughout therapy, reassures gamblers and supports their new learning process.

Only one meeting per week, however, is not enough to modify automatic behaviors that have often been acquired over several years. Thus, between therapy sessions, gamblers are invited to complete readings or written exercises. These frequent exercises prompts change that is as rapid and as long-lasting as possible. Once they involve themselves completely with this therapeutic process, gamblers significantly increase their chances of being no longer dependent on gambling. These regular exercises between meetings also increase the autonomy of the participants, who become aware of their ability to face and overcome their difficulties without the presence of a therapist.

Whatever the main reason for consulting, gamblers who undergo cognitive therapy first receive an explanation about the rational foundations of the approach and are trained to recognize erroneous thoughts or cognitions associated with the persistence of their problem. The therapist then teaches them to correct these thoughts or to find other interpretations that will help them to consider gambling more realistically and slow down their gambling behavior. Similarly, gamblers can also be invited to take concrete measures to modify behaviors that are counter-productive. This combination of cognitive and behavioral aspects is subject to description later in this book (see the section on cognitive-behavioral theory below).

The cognitive approach can be best explained to clients by using a simple model. The "ABC of emotions", a model frequently employed with patients, demonstrates the link between "A" (i.e., Activating events, situations, context), "B" (i.e., Beliefs, thoughts, cognitions, interpretations, or perceptions that a person has regarding an event or a situation), and "C" (i.e., Consequence or the emotion generated by these thoughts).

A	B	C
Events	**Interpretation**	Emotion
situations, context	cognitions, interpretations, perceptions	

The ABC of emotions is based on the premise that emotions ("C") are not directly linked to a particular event or situation ("A"). Rather, the way a person interprets a situation or event ("B") acts as a bridge between a situation ("A") and the resulting emotion ("C"). In this sense, the particular interpretation a person has of a situation influences that person's reaction to the situation; it is not the situation in itself that invariably produces a particular reaction. Furthermore, the way a person interprets a situation, and the emotions resulting from this interpretation, will in turn influence that person's behavioral reaction to the initial situation. A simple example illustrates the ABC of emotions.

Let us begin by looking at "A", the situation: Lucy runs into her friend Paul in the hallway that leads to their boss's office. She greets him warmly, but Paul only responds with a nod of the head, which is unusual for him. Paul appears withdrawn and does not smile. Now let's look at "C", the emotion. The question here is: How will Lucy react? How will she feel after running into Paul? The first thing that should be obvious is that many reactions are possible. For instance, Lucy may feel uncomfortable or she may remain completely indifferent. How can we predict which reaction she will have? That is where "B", Lucy's interpretation of the situation, comes in. Lucy may interpret the situation in several ways. For instance, she might think that Paul is angry with her. This interpretation will make Lucy feel confused and disappointed because she will not understand why Paul is angry with her. Alternatively, Lucy may attribute Paul's attitude to the fact that he is preoccupied about meeting with his boss to discuss important issues. This second interpretation allows Lucy to feel less responsible for Paul's cold attitude. Other interpretations of the situation are also possible: Lucy may attribute Paul's attitude to a difficult family situation, or to being particularly tired over the last few days. The list of possible interpretations, each of which would create a particular emotional reaction in Lucy, is endless. This example demonstrates that Lucy's reaction is not directly determined by the situation (running into Paul in this case). Rather, Lucy's reaction depends on how she interprets her encounter with her co-worker.

Regarding treatments based on the cognitive approach, some studies have shed light on how the modification or correction of erroneous perceptions can change gambling habits. Given that erroneous cognitions are not only involved in the persistence of gambling, but are directly related to the maintenance of gambling problems, they should be considered as an important target for treatments. In fact, most elements that trigger the urge to gamble are related to these kinds of erroneous beliefs and perceptions. A lack of intervention on these aspects can prejudice gamblers in their efforts to cease gambling because if they do not possess the tools to recognize and confront their own erroneous cognitions, they run a great risk of relapsing.

Even if a person has the intention to stop gambling, simply thinking that today is their "lucky day", or that they deserve to win, may lead gamblers to gamble again. That is why the approach we use favors the combination of both behavioral and cognitive interventions. Furthermore, the work to be carried out at the cognitive level requires, beforehand, that the resource person conduct a thorough assessment of the gambling problem, its consequences, and cognitions associated with gambling. The following chapter on the assessment of gamblers provides an overview of leads and effective strategies to evaluate these cognitions in detail.

During the last decade, other researchers developed a cognitive treatment and tested it on gamblers. The intervention involved explaining the cognitive model to gamblers who, with assistance, gained awareness of their erroneous cognitions about gambling. Gamblers questioned their beliefs and tested their validity by using specific information or facts, such as the probabilities of winning at gambling games.

There was then an attempt to modify certain cognitions. The idea that there exist winning strategies is challenged by concretely testing the validity of the strategies used by the gamblers. It consists of showing gamblers that other factors influence the game and that they have difficulty identifying them and even more difficulty controlling them. Many gamblers also believe that money lost can be recuperated if they play more. To modify this belief, gamblers are asked to reflect upon the fact that players generally win less than 2 out of 10 times. Gamblers also frequently believe they have good chances of winning, despite the fact that the contrary is more likely. Gamblers are thus invited to re-evaluate their estimation by considering that, on the one hand, the gains they could make would not compensate their losses and, on the other, the probabilities are very high that they will lose if they gamble, which corresponds a lot more to reality.

Gamblers also believe that their financial losses caused by gambling are minor. In order to increase gamblers' awareness of the enormity of their financial losses, the sum of losses incurred over the course of their gambling career was calculated and gamblers received tangible proof that it is indeed a major consequence of excessive gambling. In this way, gamblers benefit from concrete elements to develop a greater awareness of the financial risks associated with gambling, which will in turn help them to decide whether to gamble or not.

As can be observed, this treatment tackles several erroneous thoughts that are frequently reported by gamblers. However, the method they used to correct erroneous beliefs is not clearly known.

Our research on gambling has allowed us to better understand the cognitive aspect of gambling and to develop a specific treatment for gamblers. Our first clinical studies aimed at evaluating the effectiveness of our cognitive treatment. This treatment consists of informing gamblers about games of chance and their associated cognitive errors. It also involves correcting their erroneous perceptions and beliefs. By intervening at the cognitive level, we first seek to increase gamblers' understanding of the notion of chance. First, basic information on gambling games are provided to gamblers, particularly concerning the characteristics of chance, the independence of events, the absence of strategies, the probabilities, and the negative winning expectancy. Furthermore, we explain the notion of erroneous or inappropriate perceptions of gambling, and we present the illusion of control phenomenon as a factor that maintains gambling habits.

Gamblers learn to recognize the existence of erroneous beliefs and are encouraged to become conscious of them. As a result, they learn to detect their own erroneous thoughts on a daily basis. Once gamblers are able to recognize their erroneous thoughts as they come to mind, we help the gamblers to correct them. Finally, relapse prevention is addressed and gamblers are taught to discern situations where they are at risk of resuming their gambling habits and to implement strategies to confront these situations effectively.

We obtained good results with the few treated gamblers. We pursued our work, this time treating a greater number of gamblers and evaluating a treatment that focuses exclusively on the cognitive aspect, and obtained excellent results. We used a rigorous method that allowed us to draw reliable conclusions about the results obtained. Is it useful to comment here that very few studies have been conducted under such rigorously controlled conditions?

Cognitive-behavioral theory

While cognitive and behavioral approaches are often seen as distinct, the current tendency is to integrate the two approaches. In fact, it is within this perspective that we consider the assessment and treatment of excessive gambling throughout this book. The cognitive-behavioral approach, because it integrates both approaches, provides a much more complete explanation of the development and persistence of gambling problems.

Some investigators propose a theoretical model of gambling that is mainly based on the cognitive-behavioral approach. This theoretical model describes the potential influence of cognitive factors gambling, as well as the gamblers' need to escape and the mechanism by which these factors contribute to the appearance and development of gambling problems.

Within this theoretical model, gambling is associated with two types of reinforcement: intermittent monetary gain and physiological activation. These two reinforcers explain in part why and how gambling habits are acquired and maintained. More specifically, intermittent gains foster the belief that it is possible to make substantial wins. These wins can also give rise to a variety of erroneous cognitions about gambling and encourage the persistence to gamble.

Two types of triggering elements in a gambling session are also defined: internal elements (physiological activation, cognitions about gambling) and external elements (situations, location, time). On the one hand, gamblers become victims of their desire to gamble; more specifically, they are not able to control their erroneous thoughts, to postpone their decision to gamble, and to solve their problems. This absence or poor development of these kinds of skills predispose gamblers to contracting an abusive gambling habit. On the other hand, the events that occur during a gambling session, like wins and losses, are associated with erroneous cognitions and frequent returns to gambling activities in an attempt to recover money lost, thus contribute to the progressive increases of the frequency of gambling. This increase in the frequency of gambling inevitably leads to financial losses. In addition to monetary losses, other losses accumulate, which touch upon different spheres of gamblers' lives, such as being fired, break-ups, friends who distance themselves, etc. Instead of decreasing the love of gambling, these numerous consequences work together to maintain it.

The theory that is at the basis of the preceding model is particularly interesting because it addresses gambling according to a multi-dimensional approach, while integrating both cognitive and behavioral elements. The elements that make up the theory are not static, but interactive, which seems a lot more representative of reality.

Other cognitive-behavioral hypotheses emphasize that certain gamblers, over the course of their family experiences and throughout their interpersonal relationships, developed feelings of inadequacy and that gambling counteracts this self-deprecating feeling. According to these hypotheses, gamblers first experience feelings of inferiority, inadequacy, uselessness, and rejection from parents or their social network during childhood and adolescence, and by gambling they can temporarily attenuate or extinguish this negative image of themselves. Through gambling, gamblers flee reality and adopt a more positive image of themselves, to the point of feeling important and admired. In fact, many gamblers believe that gambling makes them more important and provides them with a more valuable social identity.

Finally, without necessarily emphasizing experiences in the first years of life, some authors suggest that gamblers feel the need to escape the realities of daily life because they are extremely anxious and unable to deal with stress, conflicts or personal difficulties. Thus, gambling relieves their stressors and quickly appears to them as a preferred solution to support them or attenuate stress, tensions, and life crises. Gamblers become full of the feeling of being powerful and admired, which reinforces their behavior and insidiously drives them to become addicted to gambling. From then on, gambling causes new problems that they are unable to overcome. They gamble both to escape and to find a solution to their financial difficulties. Paradoxically, they only get worse. The situation gradually gets out of control and their dependency on gambling becomes complete.

The behavioral chain of excessive gambling

In order to better grasp excessive gambling within a cognitive-behavioral perspective, we have broken down the relevant gambling behaviors into steps. These steps are collectively referred to as the behavioral chain of excessive gambling, which helps to explain gambling problems at both the cognitive and behavioral levels, and describes the progression towards loss of self-control when gambling. Schematically, Figure 2.1 shows the model that we use with gamblers.

A situation or event marks the first step in the chain. The urge to gamble always surfaces within a particular context, situation or circumstances that intensifies the desire to gamble. This context, which is usually a risky situation, generates risky thoughts that activate the urge to gamble. Once captured in the potential gambler's mind, this urge to gamble is fostered and maintained by various thoughts and beliefs about gambling. Here are a few examples of risky thoughts that might trigger a gambling episode: "I thought about it a lot and I think I found a better way of playing"; "I have the right to have fun once in a while"; "I'll play $20 and then I'll stop"; "I won't play more than $10. It's not a big deal. It's just for the thrill"; "Luck may be on my side tonight. I should at least check".

Once the desire to gamble is awakened, the following step in the behavioral chain corresponds to exposure to gambling. The desire to gamble might also surface only when the gambler is exposed to a gambling situation. This means that an unexpected visit to a gambling establishment or the mere sight of a game may trigger thoughts about gambling that had, until then, not crossed the gambler's mind. For instance, a person may go to a bowling alley with the sincere intention of just bowling. However, the mere sight of video lottery machines in the adjacent bar may be enough to provoke the urge to gamble.

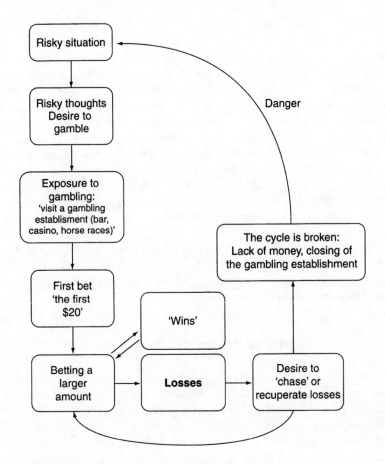

Figure 2.1: The behavioral chain of excessive gambling.

After exposure to gambling comes the bet, particularly the betting of a rather large amount. This is the third step in the chain. Gamblers generally begin a gambling session by betting small amounts of money, often to test the game, but quickly begin to bet larger sums. The subsequent steps relate to either an occasional win or a loss. For excessive gamblers, the first bet almost inevitably involves spending a larger amount. If they win occasionally, they will end up losing because of a negative winning expectancy, particularly if they gamble regularly. Furthermore, gamblers entertain other thoughts and beliefs throughout the gambling session that foster their urge to gamble, but they too are erroneous: "I think I'll change tables because this dealer isn't lucky"; "I just won a little ... I think that the machine is beginning to pay off. I should keep playing".

The last two steps in the behavioral chain concern the desire to chase or recuperate losses, and a more or less long period of abstinence from gambling. The desire to recuperate losses is a central aspect in the maintenance of gambling problems since it always draws the person back to gambling and only amplifies his or her financial loss. Prisoners of a vicious cycle, gamblers try to recuperate their losses, but only get even deeper into their financial problems. Thus, the financial problems themselves become elements that trigger gambling episodes. Again, before and after these efforts, gamblers, who are often unhappy, have new risky thoughts. "If I could win a large amount, I would stop gambling"; "I wasn't lucky. I should never have changed my strategy"; "I hate myself for having lost control. I should be able to control myself the way others can".

This vicious cycle is momentarily broken when it is simply no longer possible to gamble. Diverse reasons break the charm, such as lack of money or the closing of the gambling establishment, or the obligation to distance oneself for outside reasons. This period of abstinence can last a long time, but remains dangerous because it usually ends when another risky event or context occurs.

Cognitive-behavioral treatments

Treatments based on the cognitive-behavioral approach are diverse, but they also share many similarities. How the treatment is explained, or the links between their different elements, varies as a function of each model. However, all models include ideas that are directly linked to one another. Some cognitive-behavioral treatments emphasize the difficulty that gamblers experience when dealing with intense emotions and solving their problems. Erroneous thoughts about gambling, in combination with negative self-images, feelings of powerlessness before problems, and a lack of personal resources are four elements that are frequently observed among excessive gamblers and thus appear to be conditions associated with the appearance, development and persistence of gambling problems.

The "ABC of emotions" that was previously described clearly illustrates how one's way of thinking can influence both emotions and behavioral reactions. We have also previously discussed the fact that gamblers' erroneous thoughts about gambling nurture their desire to gamble. However, gamblers often lack tools that would simply enable them to perceive gambling more realistically. Consequently, their erroneous cognitions inevitably end up driving them to gamble again.

Cognitive-behavioral therapy for excessive gambling essentially aims to help excessive gamblers to understand all the facets of their problem in order to remedy it. The treatment thus helps them to cease gambling and deal with the many consequences of excessive gambling. Gamblers become aware of their risky thoughts while learning to correct them, and come to a better understanding of the diverse factors that determine their persistence to gamble. Close collaboration between gamblers and their therapists is required since ready-made solutions that need only be applied are not being offered. On the contrary, by questioning and scrutiny, trial and error, gamblers are guided towards discovering solutions that are appropriate for them. The exercises carried out during therapy allow gamblers to acquire or develop skills or attitudes they can then apply in daily life. These exercises will also assist gamblers to master difficult situations and counter their desire to gamble. Finally, gamblers' self-esteem improves through their appreciation of the effectiveness of the process they underwent to cease gambling.

Researchers have developed a treatment whose objective was to increase gamblers' awareness of the factors that influence their behavior. Gamblers are first asked to observe what, in their daily life, seems linked to their desire to gamble. Gamblers are then initiated to relaxation techniques to enable them to deal more calmly with risky situations. Next, they are progressively exposed to gambling, first in imagination, and then in real life. This step is a learning experience during which gamblers practice dealing with risky situations. Finally, after these experiences, gamblers' erroneous thoughts concerning gambling are corrected. While this treatment has only been tested on a small number of gamblers, it seems to have yielded satisfactory results.

We, too, have developed a treatment based on the cognitive-behavioral model presented earlier. The program, which aims for complete abstinence from gambling, has benefited adults and a few adolescents. This program includes five main components and will be described in detail in the following chapters.

In addition to informing gamblers about games of chance, their perceptions about gambling are corrected to promote a more realistic vision of gambling. Gamblers who correct, little by little, their erroneous thoughts about gambling thus become aware of the important role they play in their decision to gamble or not. For certain gamblers, it may even be necessary to offer some form of teaching and exercises focusing on problem solving, particularly for those who have difficulty dealing with their problems and who use gambling as a means of escape.

This problem-solving training helps gamblers to acquire and consolidate a realistic attitude towards gambling. By learning to recognize difficult or risky situations, and to refrain from reacting impulsively, gamblers can confront and overcome these situations. Gamblers are in fact encouraged to choose and participate in new activities that are likely to replace gambling – especially those that reproduce the positive feelings associated with gambling, such as stimulation, relaxation, and pleasure.

Given that there is a frequent link between a person's addictive problems and difficulty in expressing and asserting their feelings and needs, we offer to those in need some social skills training that relates to gambling problems. More specifically, we aim to improve the gamblers' assertiveness, which sometimes helps them to reduce their gambling activities and reinforce behaviors that lead to abstinence. Through examples and role play, gamblers learn to distinguish between the main types of interpersonal communication (passive, affirmative, aggressive, and manipulative) and recognize the importance of appropriately communicating their needs and feelings.

The final treatment component is relapse prevention, in which we attempt to question and modify gamblers' beliefs about an eventual relapse. Gamblers must understand that a relapse is not a treatment failure and does not have irreversible consequences, but is a normal reaction from which it is possible to learn. De-dramatization of gamblers' relapses and the application of concrete strategies to react to possible relapse contribute to the maintenance of treatment benefits and reduce the risk that gamblers will experience a complete relapse. Different tactics are thus examined with gamblers in order to decrease their vulnerability to certain risky situations.

Our treatment, lasting around 15 one-hour long weekly sessions, has proved to be very effective. Following treatment, 80% of participants no longer present the characteristics of excessive gamblers.

In the last few years, Spanish researchers have also tested the effectiveness of diverse cognitive-behavioral techniques. One of these treatments, which consisted of six one-hour individual sessions, focused on exercising stronger control over personal finances. Accompanied by a resource person, gamblers were exposed to gambling situations and, at the same time, learned to resist their desire to gamble. Another treatment, which also consisted of six one-hour weekly group sessions, focused on correcting erroneous cognitions. One of the advantages of the group treatment was that it gave gamblers the opportunity to share their difficulties regarding gambling and, collectively, to seek solutions to their problem. Furthermore, erroneous thoughts about gambling were collectively identified and corrected in the group. Finally, other gamblers profited from a combination of the two treatments by participating in both individual and group sessions, which involved two sessions a week during a six-week period. When all three treatments were evaluated, it was found that individual and group therapy were equally effective.

Treatments for gambling that are based on the cognitive-behavioral model thus seem to be most promising, but, as in other approaches, new studies are needed to evaluate the effectiveness of the techniques in more depth.

Eclectic treatments

Many establishments offer treatments for excessive gambling, similar to those offered to people suffering from an addiction (alcohol or drugs). These treatments, involve both individual and group sessions in addition to regular attendance at Gamblers Anonymous (GA) sessions. When combined with therapy, attending support groups (which will be discussed shortly) help excessive gamblers to reach their objective of ceasing to gamble and maintaining abstinence.

Other treatments, which seek to determine the factors that cause gamblers to lose control, combine individual interviews with sessions devoted to familial and relationship issues. Group meetings have the objective of acquiring and improving interpersonal communication skills. Some therapies also associate individual meetings and group sessions with reading, films, information sessions, participation in support groups, and family meetings. Although many gamblers assert that group therapy is the most helpful aspect of treatment, eclectic therapies usually do not provide enough information about the sessions' content, and are vague and poorly documented.

Gamblers Anonymous

Gamblers Anonymous (GA) was founded in California in 1957. It is one of the most well-known and most frequently used resources for excessive gamblers. This organization, which was inspired by Alcoholics Anonymous, functions according to the same principles. Gamblers meet on a weekly basis, discuss their gambling problems, and support each other in order to stop gambling or remain abstinent. By participating in GA meetings, gamblers can open up, even relate to other gamblers who are experiencing or have experienced the same things, thus decreasing their feelings of isolation.

Gamblers Anonymous is essentially based on the medical model – in other words, its members see gambling as an irreversible disease and promote total abstinence. Gamblers who join undertake a 12-step program during which gamblers reflect on their problem and modify their behavior. Although these 12 steps may be familiar to many, they are presented below.

1. *We admitted we were powerless over gambling – that our lives had become unmanageable.*
2. *We came to believe that a Power greater than ourselves could restore us to a normal way of thinking and living.*
3. *We made a decision to turn our will and our lives over to the care of this Power of our own understanding.*
4. *We made a searching and fearless moral and financial inventory of ourselves.*
5. *We admitted to ourselves and to another human being the exact nature of our wrongs.*
6. *We were entirely ready to have these defects of character removed.*
7. *We humbly asked God (of our understanding) to remove our shortcomings.*
8. *We made a list of all persons we had harmed and became willing to make amends to them all.*
9. *We make direct amends to such people wherever possible, except when to do so would injure them or others.*
10. *We continued to take personal inventory and when we were wrong, promptly admitted it.*
11. *We sought through prayer and meditation to improve our conscious contact with God as we understood Him, praying only for knowledge of His will for us and the power to carry that out.*
12. *Having made an effort to practice these principles in all our affairs, we tried to carry this message to other compulsive gamblers.*

According to GA, success is complete abstinence from gambling for a period of at least two years. GA groups are a very important resource for gamblers who, quite often, find comfort and understanding within them.

As with other forms of treatment, GA has a high dropout rate. Generally, members who remain faithful to GA have a positive impression of their first meeting, identify more easily with group members, feel they have been quickly counseled and assisted, feel understood, and see themselves as being able to be quickly counseled and assisted. On the other hand, participants who drop out are those who perceive the program more negatively and believe that their gambling problem is less serious than that of the others, which might explain why some participants have difficulty identifying with group members. Moreover, participants who drop out are generally younger than the average age of group members and are often unemployed; they seldom participate voluntarily and do in fact have a less severe gambling problem. Finally, according to some studies, GA meetings are much more effective for gamblers who have intense family, interpersonal, professional and financial difficulties, and who have had fewer or no relapses, but for whom the gambling problem has reached a critical stage.

Conclusion

The different theoretical models of excessive gambling discussed here offer some understanding of gambling problems. However, several models remain incomplete and only partly explain how the problems appear and develop. Erroneous perceptions about gambling – the need to escape, stimulation seeking, contextual aspects, biological factors, and personal characteristics – are all important elements in explaining gambling problems. Few studies and very little research have been able to evaluate these theoretical models adequately. While research has evolved over the past years and some aspects are better defined today, many questions remain unanswered. The same can be said of the treatment of excessive gambling. Too few studies have evaluated their effectiveness using a rigorously controlled methodology. Nonetheless, cognitive-behavioral treatments seem to offer the most promising results and interesting therapeutic avenues. Before turning our attention to the treatment of excessive gamblers, let us look at how to assess and identify gamblers' gambling habits.

3

ASSESSING THE GAMBLER

The majority of excessive gamblers who seek treatment do so when their problem has reached a critical stage. At this point, not only have gamblers used up the last of their resources, but are struggling with the numerous negative consequences of their excessive gambling. When gamblers agree to consult a professional, it is fairly easy to recognize their problem. However, recognition of a gambling problem is only part of the assessment because, in addition to diagnosis, many related aspects warrant examination. A detailed assessment of gamblers enables the therapist to determine the severity of the gambling problem with regards to frequency and intensity, while taking into account the consequences experienced by the gambler and those around him. Furthermore, it will be easier for the resource person or therapist to develop a treatment plan as well as determine a prognosis if gamblers' motivation to undergo the process, as well as their expectations and objectives, are carefully examined.

This chapter describes the main instruments employed to assess the gambling process, as well as the different factors to explore during the assessment of an excessive gambler. We will limit ourselves to aspects specific to gambling. If readers are interested in exploring other facets of excessive gambling, such as anxiety or depression, they can easily find publications specializing in these topics elsewhere.

Diagnostic instruments for excessive gambling

The characteristics and criteria defining pathological gambling are described in the *Diagnostic and Statistical Manual of Mental Disorders* (DSM-IV), which is published by the American Psychiatric Association. Pathological gambling is listed under "Impulse control disorders not elsewhere classified" and is defined as persistent and recurrent maladaptive gambling that interferes with personal, family, or occupational functioning.

The ten criteria of the American Psychiatric Association

The ten criteria established by the American Psychiatric Association are the main instrument used to diagnose excessive gambling. This document can be used to obtain precious information regarding gambling-related behaviors, as well as the severity of gambling habits. Furthermore, examination of the gambling problem according to these criteria shed light on the consequences of gambling in different spheres of gamblers' lives: family, occupational, social, academic, financial, and legal. Note that at least five of the ten criteria listed in Box 3.1 must be met for a diagnosis of pathological gambling.

Box 3.1   DSM-IV criteria for pathological gambling

1. The gambler is preoccupied with gambling (e.g., preoccupied with reliving past gambling experiences, handicapping or planning the next venture, or thinking of ways to get money with which to gamble).

2. The gambler needs to gamble with increasing amounts of money in order to achieve the desired excitement.

3. The gambler has had repeated unsuccessful efforts to control, cut back, or stop gambling.

4. The gambler is restless or irritable when attempting to cut back or stop gambling.

5. The gambler gambles as a way of escaping from problems or of relieving a dysphoric mood (e.g., feelings of helplessness, guilt, anxiety, depression).

6. After losing money gambling, the gambler often returns another day to get even (i.e., "chasing" one's losses).

7. The gambler lies to family members, his therapist, or others to conceal the extent of involvement with gambling.

8. The gambler has committed illegal acts such as forgery, fraud, theft, or embezzlement to finance gambling.

9. The gambler has jeopardized or lost a significant relationship, job, or educational or career opportunity because of gambling.

10. The gambler relies on others to provide money to relieve a desperate financial situation caused by gambling.

Examination of these criteria

The assessment of gamblers according to the ten criteria in Box 3.1 enables a gambling problem to be clearly identified. Even if there often is no doubt that we are in the presence of an excessive gambler, it is useful to have a precise idea of the number of criteria met, especially when a second assessment is necessary. In fact, certain circumstances require a reassessment of the gambling problem shortly after treatment. It is easier to determine the extent of progress a person makes by comparing the number of criteria met upon initial assessment and the number of criteria met after treatment. For instance, such an assessment would be conducted on an excessive gambler who was incarcerated and wishes to obtain conditional release. Furthermore, if a gambler lost her job because of gambling, her employer can decide whether to re-hire her if she demonstrates a real change in her behavior. In such contexts, criteria from this diagnostic manual help to quantify and objectify changes in gamblers.

The following sections consist of an in-depth analysis of these diagnostic criteria. Note that determining whether a criterion is met sometimes meets with ambiguity or difficulties. In such cases, it is helpful to reformulate the question in such a way as to obtain a clear and precise response, and to conduct a rigorous assessment of the problem. At all times, the therapist's clinical judgment should determine the accuracy and weight of "responses" to these criteria.

Sometimes, assessment according to these ten diagnostic criteria is problematic, particularly in relation to events that took place in the past. The assessment is conducted as a function of the present time, examining the period during which assessment is conducted. Many criteria are generally not problematic, given that it is easier to respond to questions related to the present tense, as can be observed in the following examples. For instance: Is the gambler presently preoccupied by gambling? Does he or she have a tendency to increase his or her wagers? Do his or her efforts to cease gambling make him or her irritable and agitated? Does he or she return to gamble on a regular basis in order to recuperate money he or she has lost? Does he or she lie in order to camouflage the severity of his or her gambling problem?

All things considered, the resource person will probably have no difficulty in determining whether the gambler meets those criteria. But assessment of the remaining criteria can be more difficult. We take care to make specific comments on these issues in the detailed description of the ten criteria listed below.

A description of the criteria according to the American Psychiatric Association

1. *The gambler is preoccupied with gambling (e.g., preoccupied with reliving past gambling experiences, handicapping or planning the next venture, or thinking of ways to get money with which to gamble).*

The first criterion refers to preoccupation with gambling. It is very uncommon for excessive gamblers to not meet this criterion. In fact, as gambling problems worsen, they become a central focus of gamblers' lives. Gamblers therefore spend a lot of time thinking about their prior losses, as well as the few substantial gains, which they especially remember. Both their losses and wins maintain their desire to gamble since they contemplate recuperating money lost or even repeating their wins. They plan their next gambling session or take certain steps to find money with which to gamble again. Gamblers occasionally report experiencing a strong desire to gamble throughout the entire day. Thus, we determine the extent to which gambling is present in gamblers' minds, for example, by asking them to estimate the number of days per week, or the number of hours per day, they think about gambling. Some gamblers find it easier to estimate the percentage of time spent thinking about gambling or engaging in gambling-related activities such as studying horse race programs or calling people to borrow a sum of money that they secretly invest into gambling.

For the majority of gamblers, preoccupation with gambling represents a veritable obsession. Among the examples that some have related to us, the night preceding the arrival of a sum of money in the mail has sometimes been marred by insomnia and tremors. It is also common to hear of gamblers who compulsively check their mailbox until the mail is delivered. Others report dreaming about diverse gambling scenarios, both happy and sad, on nights following a period of intense gambling. Finally, some gamblers have reported constantly thinking about tricks or strategies, hoping one day to find the winning combination or sequence.

Some gamblers may report not being constantly preoccupied by gambling. Indeed, their preoccupation may be temporary or time-limited. For instance, a person on welfare who has no other income can, once each month, experience an intense desire to gamble and have frequent thoughts about gambling prior to receiving the monthly welfare check. After having lost a great amount of money gambling, this person may see his obsession rapidly extinguish, only to resurface the following month. Knowing that he will not receive any money for the rest of the month, the gambler is relieved and the tension he experienced decreases or becomes latent. Although in this last case, the gambler does not continuously think about gambling, this first criterion should be considered as met since the preoccupation with gambling manifests itself as a function of his access to money.

2. *The gambler needs to gamble with increasing amounts of money in order to achieve the desired excitement.*

The second criterion refers to the monetary dimension of gamblers' behavior, particularly with regards to monetary risk-taking behavior during gambling. Gamblers seek an optimal level of stimulation and will progressively increase their wagers throughout a gambling period or from one session to another. Since the gambling problem develops progressively, the sums of money bet often shed some light on this evolution.

When questioning gamblers about their gambling behaviors, we verify whether they tend to increase the amount of their wagers or to take greater financial risks in order to attain the desired level of excitement. For instance, a gambler may report being unable to keep to small wagers while playing video lottery or slot machines. On the contrary, he rapidly increases the amounts being bet during a same gambling session. Similarly, a Blackjack amateur may report that he no longer behaves as he did when he first started gambling and that he no longer gambles at tables whose minimal bet is 5 dollars, but when he enters the casino he goes directly to the tables where the initial wager is $10 or higher. Gamblers may even assert that it is not worth gambling if they only have $20 in their pocket. Previously, $20 was enough, but today they will not even bother going to the casino if they do not have at least $100 or $200 in their wallet (or even more). In their eyes, they have better chances of winning if they begin by wagering a larger amount of money. Moreover, gamblers who have used up their financial resources will sometimes decide to gamble with the little money they have left. However, these people will easily admit that they will wager a greater sum of money as soon as it becomes available.

If gamblers admit to generally increasing their wagers, they meet the second criterion. Many gamblers even report wagering the maximum bet throughout their entire gambling session. Such gamblers do not even perceive the possibility of gambling moderately because they would draw neither excitement nor pleasure from it, and believe that their odds of winning are considerably diminished.

3. *The gambler has had repeated unsuccessful efforts to control, cut back, or stop gambling.*

The third criterion refers to the desire to cease or diminish the intensity of gambling. Prior attempts to stop gambling are also revealed at this point. In order to meet this criterion, gamblers must have manifested the intention to change their behavior or have undertaken some steps, unsuccessfully, to cease gambling or reduce their activities to a reasonable level. It is very uncommon for excessive gamblers never to have wished to cease or limit their gambling, or never to have made any attempts to do so. For some, efforts to cease gambling transform into remorse and good intentions following a large financial loss. Each day they tell themselves that it is over, that they will gamble no more, but it is a perpetual battle since these resolutions disappear once the loss is forgotten or when new money is received.

Others have already taken steps to consult a therapist. Unfortunately, many of them fail to go through with the treatment for various reasons. For instance, they seldom finish their therapy and therefore do not give themselves the opportunity to benefit from notable clinical changes. Also, some gamblers attend therapy sessions regularly without investing themselves, thus never putting into practice the ideas or taking advantage of the instruments presented to them, which greatly diminishes the effectiveness of the therapeutic process. On the other hand, consulting a resource person who is only minimally informed about gambling problems and its treatment will greatly limit the expected positive effects. Finally, many excessive gamblers attend Gamblers Anonymous at some time. However, certain gamblers do not attend on a regular basis, while others would benefit more from individual therapy that would help them to put an end to their bad habits.

Among the efforts made and identified by gamblers, we mention either the management of personal finances by another person, or voluntarily cutting down on gambling activities, whether they take place in gambling establishments as such or elsewhere (i.e., bars, lottery counters, etc.). In fact, the idea or intention to control oneself is very powerful since many gamblers report having been convinced that they could limit themselves to wagering $20 without being able to do so.

4. *The gambler is restless or irritable when attempting to cut back or stop gambling.*

The fourth criterion refers to the psychological effects of withdrawal. Many gamblers report feeling agitated, impatient, or irritable when attempting to stop or cut back on gambling. Many refer to the image of a lion in a cage to describe what they feel when trying not to gamble. Gamblers are sometimes under the impression that by holding back or by not letting themselves gamble, they will be cheated out of a win. Often, this belief of turning their back on a lucky star or letting the jackpot slip right by them has a considerable impact on their mood. Furthermore, gamblers generally have no trouble recognizing these mood disturbances when questioned about them. Other gamblers report intense physiological reactions such as headaches, nausea, gastrointestinal problems, or trembling. One of the gamblers we treated reported afterwards being so afraid of re-experiencing the unpleasant symptoms of withdrawal that his fear motivated him to avoid risky situations, but also reassured him that he would never gamble again.

5. *The gambler gambles as a way of escaping from problems or of relieving a dysphoric mood (e.g., feelings of helplessness, guilt, anxiety, depression).*

The fifth criterion refers to the reasons that motivate a person to gamble. Sometimes, people gamble as a means of escaping anxiety-provoking difficulties, or simply to change their frame of mind when upsetting situations or events occur, such as conflicts or frustrations. Gambling is also a way for some people to appease negative moods or unpleasant feelings such as powerlessness, guilt, anxiety, anger, or sadness related to various challenges or situations. A great deal of gamblers report feeling a loss of self-control when emotional and thus are quickly swept away by gambling. Among other things, gambling creates a vacuum, an empty space within which gamblers can momentarily lose themselves, forget all of life's frustrations, and think of nothing but the game. On the other hand, other gamblers perceive their lives to be an empty hole and gamble in an attempt to fill that void.

Sometimes, the consequences of excessive gambling are so difficult to deal with that gamblers, because of a lack of appropriate resources, find themselves delving back into gambling in order to forget their problems, if only for a short time. Gamblers who meet the fifth criterion generally acknowledge that they gamble as a way of escaping problems. However, many gamblers claim that their desire to gamble is not necessarily linked to their mood, but rather that it is motivated by the desire to win money. Assessing this criterion therefore requires special attention since many gamblers seek monetary gains that would allow them to get out of a financial dilemma. For them, gambling seems like the ultimate and best solution to obtain money quickly and to solve financial difficulties; this solution is also perceived as being less risky than committing an illegal act that could have considerable consequences.

There are various reasons that motivate a person to gamble. Relationship problems, conflicts or loss of interest at work, loneliness, boredom, and financial worries are some of the numerous motivations that gamblers frequently report. An understanding of these motivating factors provides a clearer idea of the elements on which it will be necessary to insist throughout treatment.

6. *After losing money gambling, the gambler often returns another day to get even (i.e., "chasing" one's losses).*

The sixth criterion is a determining factor of excessive gambling. Almost all gamblers return to gamble on a regular basis in order to recuperate their losses. It is often at this moment that the vicious cycle of excessive gambling is set into motion. While most gamblers gamble again to recuperate their losses, the rare gambler can gamble his or her entire paycheck in one session without seeking to recuperate the money later, for lack of financial resources. Other gamblers are haunted by previous losses and they dream of winning back money lost in a previous gambling session. Sometimes, they are motivated to gamble again to recuperate their most recent loss rather than the totality of their losses. Finally, in more ambiguous cases, it may be appropriate for gamblers to specify the manner in which they attempt to recuperate their losses.

7. *The gambler lies to family members, his therapist, or others to conceal the extent of involvement with gambling.*

The seventh criterion highlights a common behavior among excessive gamblers: i.e., lying. A large number of excessive gamblers admit having lied to family members or others about the true extent of their gambling habit. They hide money that is destined for gambling activities, lie about absences or tardiness, and invent all sorts of reasons to justify their lack of money. The car breaking down or having a flat tire is a classic example used to explain being late. An extreme example of lying is that of a man who lied about having cancer and went as far as to shave his head in order to lead others to believe that he was receiving chemotherapy, while in fact he was spending all of his time gambling. Another gambler was so embarrassed about her gambling problem that she signed up for group therapy under a fake name.

Lying to camouflage a gambling problem can take various forms. However, it is false to assert that gamblers have always been liars. For most excessive gamblers, lying was not common practice before the appearance of a gambling problem. If gambling and the shame with which it is sometimes associated motivate gamblers to lie, they are often not at ease with this new behavior. On the contrary, these lies provoke great dissonance in them by being against their values.

Gamblers may also lie during assessment or therapy. For instance, gamblers may be embarrassed to admit to their loved ones or therapist that they had gambled again. Others will deliberately not divulge information about activities or illegal acts for which they often fear suffering the consequences. In fact, lying is a behavior that is almost invariably found among the majority of gamblers. Therefore, the therapist must decide if it is necessary to address contradictions and inconsistencies in the "client's" discourse. It may also be appropriate to take into consideration comments and statements from members of the gamblers' social network because people who are close to the gambler often provide the therapist with information that the gambler did not reveal. Some gamblers may ask the therapist to speak to members of their social network about facts they consider essential. Whether it is appropriate for the therapist or resource person to address certain lies or contradictions is left to their clinical judgment. While some gamblers would benefit from confrontation, such actions may hinder the therapeutic process or even endanger it.

8. *The gambler has committed illegal acts such as forgery, fraud, theft, or embezzlement to finance gambling.*

The eighth criterion refers to illegal acts committed by gamblers in order to finance their gambling habits. Gamblers are often very reticent to admit to such acts, mainly out of fear of the consequences. However, information about this subject can provide supplementary clues about the severity of the gambling problem. The therapist must adhere to identifying the types of illegal acts committed, the frequency, and the sums of money involved. It is also important for the therapist to enquire about charges brought against the gambler or current court proceedings. It is not, however, necessary for the therapist to know all the details. As mentioned above, gamblers are often reluctant to talk about any reprehensible acts they have committed. Actually, the therapist only needs to know whether illegal acts have already been committed. Generally, the little information gathered indicates the severity of the gambling problem. Furthermore, determining whether the gambler is currently at risk of committing illegal acts or of continuing to commit them, is a clinical indicator that helps to decide the extent to which one should gather more information.

Over the past years, throughout our research, a variety of illegal acts have been reported to us. For instance, one gambler reported using his company's credit card repeatedly in order to finance his gambling activities. Another gambler reported stealing computer products from his workplace and selling them to get money for gambling. Some gamblers admitted stealing from their own children by either emptying their piggy banks or withdrawing money from their bank accounts. One gambler even reported selling a cat he found in the street. Others have prostituted themselves. All these actions are often desperate acts: desperation to find money with which to gamble in order to reimburse debts. Sometimes, gamblers who have no more financial resources do anything they can to obtain some money to gamble, believing that with that money, they will win and easily be able to reimburse what they "borrowed".

How should this criterion be assessed if the illegal acts were committed long ago? In assessing the eighth criterion, special attention needs to be given to the temporal aspect. For instance, if illegal acts were repeatedly committed two or three years ago, but the gambler has not committed any since, this criterion need not be evaluated positively. In fact, despite the frequency or severity of the acts committed, what matters here is whether the gambler has stopped committing them, either because he or she decided to, or because he or she was arrested. Many gamblers have much difficulty assuming the consequences of their actions. However, being charged with an illegal act or sent to prison, for example, is not enough to consider this criterion to be met if the gambler has not committed reprehensible acts for a long period of time.

9. *The gambler has jeopardized or lost a significant relationship, job, or educational or career opportunity because of gambling.*

The ninth criterion refers to familial, academic, social, and professional consequences of excessive gambling. Has the gambler endangered or lost a significant relationship with a romantic partner, child, or friend? Is gambling interfering with his or her job or studies? If so, how? To what extent?

Clearly defining the consequences of gambling provides useful clues about the severity of the gambling problem. For instance, gambling can cause the loss of employment since employers must do something when they discover that their employee financed his gambling activities with expense account money. Similarly, an employee who works as a delivery person, but spends many working hours gambling makes his employer lose a lot of money and thereby jeopardizes his employment. Moreover, close friends and family may stop trusting or break off relationships with the gambler because of lying and repeated absences. Obviously, the consequences are as numerous as they are varied, but proper assessment helps to establish a plan of action by determining life spheres that can be addressed by particular interventions.

A more precise assessment of when these consequences occurred or whether the negative repercussions are currently being experienced allows the therapist to estimate the severity of the problem at the time of assessment and during the months that preceded it. It is the period during which the gambler experienced the said difficulties that will determine whether the criterion is met. For instance, if a gambler has had a recent romantic break up or recently lost his or her job and is still in a period of reorganization following either of these events, the criterion would be met. Whatever the case may be, the therapist must base his or her decision about whether the gamblers is *currently* affected by these difficulties on clinical judgment.

10. *The gambler relies on others to provide money to relieve a desperate financial situation caused by gambling.*

The tenth criterion refers to financial consequences of excessive gambling. Because of a financial situation that is most often disastrous, gamblers frequently seek the financial support of people around them. Many gamblers depend on the positive feelings of friends and family who often cannot tolerate one of their own having financial difficulties and thus accept to pay off their gambling debts. While the majority of gamblers exhaust their social networks, others borrow from the bank or from loan sharks, and even place themselves in dangerous situations. Others leave personal objects with brokers in exchange for money they will then gamble.

How can this criterion be assessed for gamblers who have taken loans in the past? To assess the tenth criterion, the moment when loans were made warrants consideration. For instance, if the gambler received financial aid from others shortly before assessment, the criterion would be met. Again, the therapist must rely on his or her clinical judgment when deciding whether this criterion is met.

Conclusion

These diagnostic criteria are among the most used diagnostic instruments worldwide. However, despite its current wide use, this instrument has certain flaws. First, these criteria were developed by a group of researchers and clinicians that do not specialize in gambling. This may partially explain why the criteria sometimes lack specificity. The diagnostic criteria for problem gambling are very similar to those for addictive disorders (alcohol, drugs, etc.). As these two disorders have many common characteristics, it is difficult to understand why excessive gambling is not listed in the category of addictions rather than in the category of impulse control disorders. When compared to diagnostic criteria for substance-dependence disorders, the criteria for excessive gambling are not associated with a scale of severity. For substance-dependence disorders, there are three degrees of dependence: mild, moderate, and severe. Moreover, six other specifiers are also used to define the evolution of the disorder: early full or partial remission, sustained full or partial remission, on medication, or in a controlled environment. If all these specifiers were added to excessive gambling criteria, they would, without a doubt, help to better define the severity and evolution of problem gambling for particular individuals.

In evaluating excessive gamblers using these ten criteria, the resource person must consider each of these criteria in a dichotomous manner (i.e., present or absent). Accordingly, the decision made can be very subjective, to the extent that two therapists evaluating the same gambler may arrive at different scores. In sum, the criteria lack details and scrutinize certain dimensions in such a way that they are not as efficacious as the therapist would like. For instance, there are no specifications regarding the intensity, frequency, and duration of certain behaviors. Moreover, the lack of a temporal index provokes much confusion when reassessing gamblers according to the same criteria at a later date. Finally, although a gambling problem is essentially a financial problem, or at least one that generates financial consequences, it is quite astonishing to note that only one criterion deals with this aspect. Therefore, there is a need to develop other diagnostic instruments that are more specific and more precise. Presently, combining these diagnostic criteria with other instruments allows for a more precise assessment of excessive gambling.

The South Oaks Gambling Screen

If the ten criteria of the American Psychiatric Association are considered to be the main diagnostic instrument, a questionnaire called the South Oaks Gambling Screen (SOGS) is presented as a complementary instrument. (The questionnaire and scoring sheet are available in Appendix 1.) The SOGS, which is mainly used in epidemiological and clinical studies, is an interesting and practical instrument for detecting gambling problems. Moreover, the SOGS enables the therapist to obtain detailed information on gambling habits and provides additional information on various topics such as preferred games, gambling frequency, or methods of obtaining money with which to gamble. The SOGS is typically administered to gamblers during their first therapy session. We complete the SOGS with the gambler during our first telephone conversation, using a version that was made for telephone interviewing.

The maximum score on the SOGS is 20 points. According to its authors, a score of 3 or 4 indicates a potential gambling problem, whereas a score of 5 or more indicates a probable gambling problem. Furthermore, a score of 9 or more indicates a severe gambling problem. However, a person who uses this questionnaire alone to arrive at a diagnosis should be warned about interpreting the scores. Our studies have shown that this assessment instrument overestimates the number of excessive gamblers. Given the high number of false positives, it is preferable to use a second instrument, such as the ten criteria of the American Psychiatric Association, to validate the diagnosis. In fact, no diagnosis should be established solely based on this questionnaire.

Among the questions asked, gamblers indicate which games they have played in their lifetimes and estimate the frequency with which they have played these games according to a specific choice of responses. Gamblers also estimate the largest sum of money that they have lost in one day, further revealing to the resource person or therapist the extent of spending related to gambling. It is worth mentioning that it is sometimes difficult for gamblers to remember certain details when the questionnaire takes them back one year or asks them to estimate, for instance, the amount of money they lost in their lifetime. The therapist can therefore only expect to receive estimations or approximate answers to these questions unless gamblers have kept a detailed register of their gambling activities, which is extremely unlikely. Therefore, it may be preferable to ask gamblers to make a more realistic estimation, by calculating, for example, the amount of money spent on gambling on a monthly or weekly basis.

This questionnaire also enables the assessment of gambling-related behaviors, such as returning to gamble in order to recuperate prior losses and lying about involvement with gambling. Gamblers also estimate the frequency with which they engage in these behaviors. Other behaviors are also assessed: gambling more money than intended, missing work or school in order to gamble, and borrowing money to gamble. Along the same lines, gamblers are also asked about the existence of non-reimbursed debts. With the assistance of the questionnaire's response choices, the therapist is able to collect information regarding the places, as well as by what intermediaries and methods gamblers obtain money with which to gamble.

This questionnaire also provides precious clues about the relationship between gamblers and their friends and family, more specifically regarding gambling habits. Gamblers indicate whether people close to them have criticized their gambling habits, and if the way they manage their personal finances or family budget has created conflicts, especially with regards to gambling. Furthermore, it is also important to know whether their parents currently have a gambling problem or had one in the past. Finally, gamblers are asked to make a verdict about their behavior: Do they think they have a gambling problem? Given that many gamblers deny the existence of such a problem, their answer to this question provides important information.

In parallel with the diagnosis of excessive gambling, which is conducted with the assistance of specific instruments, several other dimensions of excessive gambling need to be assessed in detail. Proper assessment of these dimensions will not only allow gamblers to better understand their problem, it will also guide the resource person in his or her therapeutic work. Remember that a score of 5 or more is a strong indication of a probable excessive gambling problem.

Identifying motives for consulting

The reasons that motivate gamblers to consult a professional vary from one individual to another. Specifying what these reasons are provides precious indications regarding gamblers' motivation to engage in a thera-peutic process, as well as their intentions to stop gambling. Many ques-tions about reasons for consulting can be asked: Why are you consulting now? In what context? Has a particular event precipitated your decision to seek treatment? Gamblers who seek therapy for preventive measures are rare. Most often, a key event precipitates gamblers' decision to consult, during a period when they do not foresee any other solutions. For instance, following a substantial monetary loss, gamblers sometimes feel helpless and seek ways to cease gambling. On other occasions, it is their inability to reimburse debts that raises their awareness of the severity of their gambling problem and motivates them to consult. Problems at work, as well as marital and family conflicts, are also among the motives that are frequently reported by gamblers who consult a professional.

It is also common for gamblers to give in to the pressures of people in their social network. The therapist may choose to explore this aspect. For whom is the gambler seeking treatment? Is the gambler consulting to satisfy the demands of an exasperated employer or wife? Is the gambler seeking treatment as part of a court requirement to undergo therapy to treat his or her gambling problem? Is the gambler doing it to clear his or her conscience? To what extent is the gambler's desire to stop gambling for the sake of others greater than his or her desire to stop gambling for personal reasons? Whatever the gambler's reasons for seeking assistance to solve a gambling problem, these reasons must be examined very carefully in order to better assess the gambler's motivation to participate in therapy.

Acting for the sake of others can result in two opposite effects. Consulting a specialist while being pressured by others can puzzle some gamblers or slow down their engagement in the process, rendering the treatment less effective. On the other hand, the pressure from others can have a beneficial effect because, even if motivation is somewhat extrinsic, it can be just as effective. The therapist or resource-person can exploit this aspect to maintain motivation throughout therapy. Moreover, if a member of the family is pressuring the gambler to consult, this person can become an important resource or source of support.

Many gamblers are ambivalent when it comes time to decide to consult for a gambling problem. Often, they have difficulty imagining being able to completely stop gambling and never gamble again. How can we explain this ambivalence? Given that gambling occupies a large part of gamblers' lives, they may fear finding themselves in a distressing void. Moreover, gamblers often remember occasions when they won, and may continue to believe that they will win again and that gambling is the ideal solution to their financial problems. It is this obsession that motivates them, in part, to pursue gambling activities.

Excessive gambling specialists recognize that gamblers are ambivalent when it comes to engaging in a therapeutic process. It is crucial to know the precise reasons for consulting as well as to systematically evaluate gamblers' motivation to gamble, particularly at the beginning of treatment. Properly defining gamblers' motives to consult helps to estimate their intentions with regards to such a therapeutic process, to estimate their eventual persistence, and establish a prognosis. Gamblers may also be asked what they consider to be difficult or embarrassing: In what way is gambling found to be problematic? Why do you think you need treatment? etc.

Prior efforts to cease gambling provide information about gamblers' motivation to put an end to gambling and to engage in therapy. They also inform the resource-person about what therapeutic route to take. Has the gambler already sought treatment for his or her gambling problem or is this the first time? More specifically, what has the gambler tried in the past? Where, who, and when has the gambler consulted? These are not unimportant details; on the contrary, this information establishes the prior therapeutic tools or processes that have worked for the gambler in the past. They also bring to the front potential solutions and, most of all, allow gamblers to recognize their past successes and use them to attain their objectives. By making a list of prior efforts and specifying when, for how long, the resources used (Who? What kind of approach?), the obtained results (success, failure, dropout), as well as satisfaction regarding the methods employed, both the therapist and client can orient the treatment according to aspects which they deem to be important.

In order to better estimate gamblers' desire to change their behavior, they are invited to give their opinion on their determination to make efforts to cease gambling or to reduce gambling activities. As an example, we ask gamblers to quantify their desire to change using a scale from 0 to 10 – from "not at all" to "totally". The score obtained provides a supplementary indication of gamblers' determination. In doing so, gamblers find the opportunity to think more about their intentions with regards to therapy. Here is the scale.

Motivation to cease gambling

1. Are you ready to make efforts to cease gambling?

Yes_____   No_____

2. Desire to change: Please indicate the extent to which you would like to change your gambling behavior. Select the number that corresponds to your desire to change.

0	1 – 2 – 3	4 – 5 – 6	7 – 8 – 9	10
Not at all	A little	Moderately	A lot	Totally

3. What is your objective for change?...

The majority of gamblers rate their motivation at 8 or more during their first meeting. The resource-person will address this point later because it is common for a gambler's motivation to decrease after a certain time. There are many reasons that explain this change. For instance, gamblers who reimburse their debts instantaneously, or who gamble again and make a substantial win, sometimes underestimate their gambling problem. Some believe they are "cured". Weak motivation can slow treatment down. After a few sessions, these gamblers will no longer see the need to consult and will drop out for an undetermined length of time. If such a lack of motivation is suspected, it is useful to promptly re-evaluate it.

Gamblers' expectations also warrant reflection. What kind of treatment are they anticipating? What are their expectations towards the therapist? Given that expectations vary from one person to another, it is useful to discuss the treatment being offered during the first meeting. At that time, it is also important to talk to gamblers about their participation: the treatment requires that it be complete and intense. The ambivalence manifested by some gamblers makes it so that they exert little effort to cease gambling. They sometimes adopt a passive attitude and give the impression that they wish to be taken care of by the therapist, whom they perceive as the sole master of the therapeutic process and solely responsible for therapeutic success. It is therefore important for the therapist to clarify his or her role as well as that of the gamblers by explaining to them that a large part of the therapy's effectiveness is dependent upon each client's full participation, both during and between sessions.

The diagnostic interview for pathological gambling

History and evolution of the gambling problem

In order to cover different aspects related to the history and evolution of the gambling problem, we developed a diagnostic interview for pathological gambling. This semi-structured interview consists of 26 questions (see Appendix 2). It also contains the ten diagnostic criteria of the American Psychiatric Association, as well as sub-questions that facilitate the assessment and permit a more detailed account of answers to these criteria.

Information regarding the acquisition of gambling habits

The first questions of the interview deal with the motive to consult and the events that provoked the decision to consult a professional. The interview also enables the therapist to make an inventory of all the games of chance that gamblers played over the last year. Gamblers identify the games with which they experience difficulties controlling themselves, while estimating the duration of their problem. Gamblers also indicate whether they have ever played video or electronic games, and whether they played pinball during their childhood or adolescence. Given that many gamblers assert having won a substantial sum of money during their first gambling experiences, this interview includes a question addressing this subject; these events often correspond to the beginning of gambling on a regular basis. Finally, one question asks gamblers to indicate, if applicable, which people initiated them to gambling.

Details about the gambling problem

Gamblers will specify what, according to them, are elements that triggered their gambling problem, as well as the main reasons that motivate them to gamble. Moreover, gamblers indicate their weekly frequency of gambling in terms of days, hours, and amount of money spent on gambling. The semi-structured interview highlights the consequences of excessive gambling, particularly social, professional, and psychological dimensions. Gamblers determine the intensity with which their gambling interferes with these three facets of their lives. Other questions assess past and current suicidal ideation, as well as whether any suicide attempts have been made related to gambling. Many gamblers remember experiencing periods during which their mood became depressive and during which suicidal thoughts surfaced.

Examination of other addictions

There are many similarities between excessive gambling and other types of dependence. Moreover, the simultaneous presence of excessive gambling and another addiction is a frequently observed phenomenon. For this reason, it is very useful to know the other habits or behaviors that cause problems, that are presently "at risk", or that have caused difficulties in the past. This interview examines cigarette, drug, alcohol, and medication use. Gamblers estimate the proportion of gambling sessions during which they consumed alcohol or drugs. Other behaviors, such as the amount of time spent on the Internet, sexual activities, and frequency of purchasing consumer goods (compulsive shopping) are also assessed. Finally, this interview addresses the financial consequences of gambling.

Other relevant assessment questions

Although this interview provides information about the negative consequences of gambling, a detailed description of these consequences helps to establish a treatment plan. Asking numerous questions remains the most effective method. For instance, what consequences does gambling have on the gambler's professional activities? The resource person seeks to find out the frequency of absences and late arrivals caused by gambling, as well as to estimate the loss of productivity related to an excessive preoccupation with gambling. Is the gambler's job in jeopardy or has he or she lost it because of gambling? Is the gambler's employer aware of the gambling problem? Is the gambler's social life or family unit disrupted by gambling problems? Have certain significant relationships changed? In what way? If the gambler admits to having committed illegal acts to finance his or her gambling activities, the resource person must enquire about whether court proceedings are now taking place and the possible time before rulings are made. When is the gambler scheduled to appear in court? What sentence can be expected? What do the gambler's lawyer and probation officer have to say?

Among the negative consequences of excessive gambling, financial problems and outstanding debts are often the most important difficulties for almost all excessive gamblers. The following questions may shed some light on this subject:

- What is the gambler's income?
- What is his or her family's total revenue?
- Does the gambler have access to money besides his or her salary?
- How much are his or her living expenses (for instance, rent or mortgage payments, phone and electricity bills, car payments, food, etc.) in comparison to the amount of money that is generally spent on gambling?

A clear understanding of gamblers' financial obligations and of their living situation (e.g., does the gambler live alone or does he or she have children to take care of?) enables proper assessment of the severity of gambling excesses. Determining the percentage of money spent on gambling as a function of the gambler's revenue enables the therapist to clearly understand the extent to which the gambler is exceeding the limits of his or her financial means. A detailed understanding of incurred debts also help to assess the seriousness of the gambler's' financial difficulties.

- How much does the gambler owe overall?
- To whom does he or she owe money?
- How much does he or she owe to each of these people?
- What means has he or she thought about, or used, to manage this delicate financial situation?
- Is he or she considering filing bankruptcy, if it has not already been declared?

Once the therapist has a clear understanding of the gambler's financial difficulties, the gambler can more easily be helped to face these difficulties and guided in choosing the most realistic solutions possible. Financial difficulties are a central element of problem gambling because not only do they represent an obvious consequence of gambling excess, but they also become a key element that triggers future gambling episodes. In fact, gamblers often perceive gambling as the sole solution to their financial problem.

Assessing the presence of simultaneous addictions

In addition to their gambling problem, gamblers often have other diffi-culties like alcoholism or drug addiction. In treatment facilities for gamblers, approximately 30 to 70% of patients have an addiction to one or more substances. Obviously, these high percentages are not found in the general population, but rather among a specific population – e.g., gamblers who are consulting a professional and who are admitted to treatment facility. In fact, people who work with excessive gamblers generally expect there to be a significant proportion with more than one problem. Furthermore, the presence of a second problem renders the therapeutic process more difficult for some gamblers.

Similarly, for drugs and alcohol, the therapist is interested in the context in which the person consumes. People who gamble under the influence of drugs or alcohol are at increased risk of losing control and of exceeding their limits in time and money. It is well known, for instance, that drinking alcohol decreases the cognitive faculties of individuals who also have a tendency to minimize the consequences of their gambling. Moreover, a person who gambles again under the influence of alcohol may easily lose track of money lost or downplay losses, which increases his or her likelihood of persisting to gamble longer and suffering more severe consequences.

Thus, a detailed understanding of gamblers' habits with regards to consuming drugs or alcohol will contribute towards the identification of a more appropriate treatment plan. Does the gambler drink alcohol or take drugs? If yes, what type does he or she take? How much? How frequently? By taking an inventory of drug and alcohol habits, the therapist will determine whether or not they constitute a problem, and whether they need to be more carefully assessed.

The context in which alcohol or drugs are consumed influences the intensity of gambling. Does the gambler drink or use drugs before gambling? If yes, does he or she consume a great quantity? An affirmative answer to these two questions indicates that taking drugs or drinking alcohol are among the elements that activate the decision to gamble. If many gamblers take a first drink when they begin to gamble, drinking alcohol becomes dangerous when the quantity absorbed reaches the point where it modifies gamblers' perception and motivates them to gamble more.

If the person gambles while under the influence of alcohol or drugs, it is important to obtain information about the proportion of gambling sessions when that takes place. In fact, a gambler who gambles generally or most often while under the effects of alcohol could be considered as having an addiction to alcohol. In this case, excessive gambling behavior is intimately linked to the effects of alcohol. In such circumstances, while the seriousness or the consequences of the gambling problem are obvious, drinking is a determining element in the gambler's behavior. A first intervention focusing on drinking is thus recommended.

If the drug or alcohol addiction is not treated, at the very least in conjunction with the gambling problem, it will become difficult for gamblers to deal with their gambling problem. The therapist can either refer clients to a more appropriate resource or enroll them in two parallel treatments. Given that the treatment proposed in this book is based on the thoughts of excessive gamblers, it is preferable to ensure that the implementation of treatment and its effectiveness is not jeopardized by the use of alcohol or drugs. In sum, gamblers may experience difficulties completing the exercises to model their thoughts if their perception is clouded by the influences of alcohol or drugs.

Evaluating erroneous thoughts about gambling

The treatment of excessive gambling that is proposed in this book comprises a series of cognitive and behavioral interventions. The correction of erroneous cognitions about gambling is the central element of the treatment. Knowledge of gamblers' cognitions is therefore a prerequisite for treatment.

What, however, do we mean by gamblers' cognitions? These are any thoughts, images, or expectations that are entertained by gamblers. Gamblers' perception of gambling, their interpretation of the different events that take place during a gambling session, as well as their analysis of the situation, are all cognitions about gambling. Within the same perspective, what we refer to as erroneous cognitions (or erroneous thoughts or beliefs) are any thoughts that gamblers have that are in contradiction to the logical principles of games of chance. Actually, we have observed that although the results of gambling games are determined by chance (i.e., they are unpredictable and uncontrollable), all gamblers believe, to a certain extent, that they can influence the outcome of the game either by employing strategies or by making various observations.

Numerous thoughts specifically about gambling are verbalized by gamblers. For instance, one gambler stated that when he observes a "combination that almost won" three times in a row, he is convinced that he will soon win the jackpot. Another gambler stated that when he bets a lot of money on a video lottery machine, he persists in playing because he is convinced that the machine will soon pay out. Other erroneous thoughts make reference to gamblers' behaviors and life contexts. For instance, a gambler gives himself permission to go gambling, convinced that he will be able to control himself and to wager $5, even though it is very rare that he controls himself when gambling. Another gambler reported that, after having lost $400, he was certain that he would win the $200 he needed to make an important payment. Recognizing these erroneous thoughts will thus increase gamblers' understanding of the elements that are linked to their persistence to gamble, as well as how their gambling habits are maintained, which will in turn assist them to correct their thoughts.

Research has shown that erroneous thoughts play a very important role in the development and maintenance of gambling habits. False ideas about gambling motivate gamblers to gamble and to pursue their gambling activities, but they are generally not conscious of them. Some gamblers spontaneously express their erroneous cognitions, but most gamblers do not easily perceive the impact or the presence of this cognitive material. The therapist or resource person must discover these cognitions and help gamblers to become aware of these erroneous thoughts through the use of various techniques.

The first step towards detecting erroneous thoughts is the recognition of risky situations. Gamblers have difficulty discerning the events or contexts that give rise to a gambling session. For instance, some gamblers may begin thinking about gambling the moment they receive their paycheck or when they have to go out of town for work. Knowing the situations that trigger the urge to gamble gives access to gamblers' thoughts.

Methods and techniques for assessing cognitions

In order to have a clear idea of gamblers' cognitions, the therapist will pay special attention to cognitions that appear before gambling, as well as those that manifest themselves during and after a gambling session. Regardless of when these thoughts surface, they are harmful to gamblers and influence their gambling behaviors. Here are some examples of erroneous thoughts that occur before, during, and after gambling. Before gambling, a gambler might think: "I feel good today…what if it's my lucky day?" Then, while gambling, a gambler might think: "Numbers 10 and 12 have not come out for a long time, they should be drawn soon. I'll bet the maximum amount on these numbers." Finally, after a gambling session during which the gambler lost a lot of money, he or she might think: "If I could find $20, I could recuperate the money I just lost." Erroneous cognitions therefore differ depending on whether they occur before, during, or after a gambling session.

Two techniques, which are described below, enable the therapist to meticulously reveal and assess gamblers' cognitions. One technique consists of asking gamblers to relate past gambling experiences, particularly the most recent session. The other consists of using the downward arrow technique to access thoughts that gamblers find difficult to verbalize.

Analyzing a past gambling session

For an analysis of a gambling session, gamblers are asked to remember and relate a gambling situation, describing all thoughts they had during this session in detail. In fact, the description of a past gambling experience helps to reconstruct the chain of thoughts that led them to gamble. Furthermore, gamblers more easily recall the details of their thoughts in more recent situations. Accordingly, the therapist asks gamblers to describe, with as many details as possible, the last time they gambled. With questions, the therapist can establish the events that took place that day, the context, the elements that led to gambling, as well as the associated thoughts.

For instance, a gambler may say that the last time he gambled, the decision occurred suddenly and without any planning. When coming home from work, he intended to go directly home but felt the urge to gamble and went to a gambling establishment. To better identify the chain of events and the thoughts regarding gambling, the therapist goes over the entire day by questioning the gambler. Did the person think about gambling when he or she got up that morning? When leaving home? When arriving at work? At lunch hour? Before leaving work? This way, gamblers can establish the precise moment when the urge to gamble appeared. What exactly did they think? What were they saying to themselves at that moment?

In order to encourage gamblers' verbalizations, we use the thinking aloud method. This method consists of asking clients to freely express, without any censuring or holding back, any and all intentions, suppositions, images, and thoughts that come to mind. The therapist may at times appear to be very curious, even naïve, in order to facilitate clear and detailed verbalizations of gamblers' thoughts.

Throughout the analysis of a recent gambling session, gamblers are encouraged to talk about the context, the location, the people, the events, and all other elements that are related to their gambling behavior. For instance, a gambler may relate that he did not go to the gambling establishment to gamble, but rather to observe others gamble. He may then have exchanged a few words with a bar employee who informed him that many people had recently lost significant sums of money. Believing that he had privileged information, he was convinced that luck was on his side and began to gamble immediately. This entire context, which presented itself before gambling, influenced this person and motivated him to gamble. Gamblers are then invited to provide details about their decisions, actions, and events that occurred while gambling. They indicate the amount of their bets, describe or explain changes they made to their way of betting that night, the different choices they made and the decisions they made about gambling. If needed, the therapist asks them about their thoughts after a win or a loss. Finally, what took place after the gambling session is not neglected and gamblers are again invited to express thoughts that occurred at the end of the gambling session and during the hours that followed.

In order to illustrate a discussion between a gambler and therapist, a reproduction of a conversation is presented in the following lines. This example also demonstrates the assessment of cognitions within the framework of an analysis of a gambling session.

THERAPIST: You mentioned that you gambled yesterday. Could you tell me what happened?
GAMBLER: I played and I lost a lot.

Here, the therapist is not restricted to what the gambler says. In his comment, the gambler immediately jumps to the topic of the loss, the consequences of gambling, whereas the therapist wants to know more about the context that preceded the gambling session.

THERAPIST: At what point during the day did you start thinking about gambling?
GAMBLER: Yesterday morning.

THERAPIST: When exactly yesterday morning?

GAMBLER: Towards the end of the morning.

THERAPIST: What were you doing in the minutes immediately before you started to think about gambling?

GAMBLER: I went to get my mail.

THERAPIST: What happened then?

GAMBLER: Oh yes … I remember. I opened my mail and noticed that I had two bills to pay that I had not yet expected. I had a hot flash and started to feel very nervous.

Here the gambler puts the therapist on the trail of his feelings. The therapist could continue questioning this subject. However, the therapist adheres to the objective. Remember, the therapist wants to know the gambler's thoughts. The therapist can postpone evaluating the gambler's feeling until later and therefore continues the interrogation by enquiring about the thoughts associated with the emotion mentioned.

THERAPIST: You felt nervous when you opened your mail and noticed that you had bills to pay. Why? What did you say to yourself?

GAMBLER: I told myself that I would never have enough money by the end of the month to pay all my bills.

THERAPIST: Then what did you say to yourself?

GAMBLER: I told myself that if I gambled I could maybe make more money and be able to pay my bills.

THERAPIST: And what happened?

GAMBLER: I gambled and lost everything.

THERAPIST: And then what did you say to yourself?

GAMBLER: I was really discouraged.

Once again, the gambler spontaneously talks about the emotion he felt in that situation. The therapist recognizes the gambler's emotion and will address it later, but for the moment, the therapist continues the interrogation with the objective of assessing the gambler's cognitions.

THERAPIST: I understand that you felt badly. But, what exactly was discouraging you? What were you thinking at that moment?

GAMBLER: I was discouraged because I could not deal with having lost all of that money. I told myself that luck might turn in my favor. I had to recuperate that money. If I had had a little more money on me, I could have continued to gamble and recuperate my losses. But I didn't have any more money so I felt bad.

The gambler is a little more talkative. He now gives the therapist two new paths to follow: chance and chasing losses. In this example, the therapist chooses to address the idea of chasing losses, but keeps the first path in mind in order to come back to it later.

THERAPIST: You think that you could have been able to recuperate your losses?

GAMBLER: Absolutely! There were good chances!

THERAPIST: Oh Really? What makes you think that there were good chances?

GAMBLER: With all the money I bet, I was certain that the Roulette table would pay.

This example clearly demonstrates how the therapist is not content with simply descriptive comments from the gambler. The therapist tries to gather all the thoughts related to the context or events that preceded the gambling session. Once the thoughts that occurred before gambling are identified, the therapist then becomes interested in the events that took place and the thoughts that occurred during the gambling session itself. Here is an example of a conversation between a therapist and a gambler regarding a gambling session:

THERAPIST: You say that you arrived at the casino early in the evening. When exactly did you begin gambling?

GAMBLER: Almost immediately. I did a very quick tour to size up the playing field and to get a better idea about the ambiance. I saw people winning.

THERAPIST: What did you say to yourself at that moment?

GAMBLER: It confirmed my feeling. I felt like a winner that day. I immediately went to get fifty dollars worth of tokens.

THERAPIST: You felt like a winner? What do you mean?

GAMBLER: Yes, I woke up feeling that way. I had a good feeling, a feeling that something was going to happen.

THERAPIST: Tell me what happened next.

GAMBLER: I went near the Roulette table and took a few minutes to study the table that indicates the last numbers that came out.

THERAPIST: What does that table tell you?

GAMBLER: I was instantly able to see which numbers I should bet on. Some numbers had not come out for a long time.

THERAPIST: And what does that mean, according to you?

GAMBLER: That they should be coming out soon. They're due.

THERAPIST: What makes you say that?

GAMBLER: I noticed that when numbers have not come out for a long time, they will soon come out. It's the law of averages.

Depending on his or her intentions, the therapist has two options. The therapist can either explore the gambler's belief in the law of averages or further explore the events and thoughts present during the beginning of the gambling session. In our example, the therapist opts for the second choice, i.e., the gambler's thoughts during the gambling session.

THERAPIST: Describe the way you played. What number did you bet on first?

GAMBLER: I bet on numbers 9 and 12. These two numbers don't often come out.

THERAPIST: Did you win?

GAMBLER: Not right away, but it's like I have to take the "table's pulse" in order to be sure that I am making the right choice.

THERAPIST: What do you mean?

GAMBLER: I begin by placing small wagers and carefully observe the way and the strength with which the dealer throws the marble.

THERAPIST: Why?

GAMBLER: After a few turns, it seems to me that I can predict the number on which the marble will fall.

In this example, the gambler verbalizes very freely and expresses several erroneous ideas. The therapist supports the gambler's description of the gambling session, keeping in mind that he or she seeks to know as many of the gambler's erroneous thoughts as possible. Accordingly, all questions concerning the amounts and fluctuations in bets, wins and losses, as well as the other observations that gamblers make are useful for getting to know their thoughts. At the end of the process, the therapist will also ask about events and thoughts that occurred after the gambling session.

The downward arrow technique

With certain gamblers, it can be very difficult to assess cognitions. Although some gamblers easily verbalize their thoughts, others are convinced that no thoughts preceded their desire to gamble or their decision to do so. In these cases, it may be useful to use the downward arrow technique. This technique, which enables the therapist to have access to as much cognitive information as possible, consists of establishing a sequence of erroneous thoughts associated with a particular gambling situation using questions that focus on these very thoughts.

While staying attentive to the smallest comment about gambling, the therapist first questions the gambler about a first statement in order to identify the erroneous thoughts that might be related. If the therapist then suspects that other subjacent thoughts have not yet been expressed, the gambler will be asked to explain his or her comments. The therapists pursues his or her interrogation by using sub-questions such as "Why?" or

"What did you do then?" until he or she has attained the idea that is at the basis of all these thoughts.

The downward arrow technique thus involves detailed questioning that is necessary to gather as much cognitive material as possible. Special attention must be made to any comment the gambler makes about gambling in order to throw it back and help the gambler to focus on the chain of events. Therefore, the therapist is able to make the thoughts that accompany the gambler throughout a gambling session emerge from his or her conscious; thoughts that are often masked by the memory of events only. Since the application of treatment and its effectiveness rests upon the precise recognition of cognitions, the therapist should never take a thought for granted without verifying whether the gambler is hiding one or many erroneous thoughts. It is the only route that the therapist or resource person can take to reach the objective.

In order to provide you with a concrete example of the downward arrow technique, we present an analysis of a gambling session during which the therapist uses this technique and where sub-questions follow one another until the therapist has obtained a precise portrait of all the erroneous thoughts attached to a particular false idea.

THERAPIST: You said that you wager very little at the beginning of a gambling session. Why do you do that?
GAMBLER: I want to test the video lottery machine.

From the beginning of the conversation, the therapist suspects that the gambler entertains the belief that she can control the outcome of the game. The therapist therefore tries to make the gambler verbalize this belief more explicitly.

THERAPIST: What do you mean by testing the machine?
GAMBLER: If the machine pays from the beginning, you know that it will continue to pay.
THERAPIST: What makes you think that?
GAMBLER: I noticed that the machine goes though cycles.
THERAPIST: How did you notice that?
GAMBLER: Often, it pays several times in a row and I tell myself that I shouldn't change machines.
THERAPIST: Why?
GAMBLER: I would be stupid to hand over my luck to someone else!
THERAPIST: Why do you say that?
GAMBLER: I won several times. I knew I was on the right track.
THERAPIST: Why would you say the machine was on the right track?
GAMBLER: When the wins are close together, it's a good sign.
THERAPIST: Why?

GAMBLER: Ask any gambler. They will tell you that the first bets determine the rest of the game.

THERAPIST: Why?

GAMBLER: If I win at the beginning, I am almost certain to win again. I know that I will win more money.

As can been seen in the preceding lines, the gambler has an erroneous thought regarding the cyclical functioning of video lottery machines. Thanks to the downward arrow technique, the therapist was able to obtain a clear verbalization of the underlying erroneous thoughts entertained by the gambler.

In some cases, it is even more difficult to get gamblers to express their cognitions. In the following example, the downward arrow technique helps the therapist to gain access to these erroneous thoughts.

THERAPIST: What made you decide to gamble?

GAMBLER: I suddenly had the urge to gamble and simply did so.

THERAPIST: What were you thinking about before you got there?

GAMBLER: I wasn't thinking about anything. Everything just happened so quickly. The urge was simply stronger than me and I headed out to gamble.

THERAPIST: Did something happen prior to you getting this urge?

GAMBLER: Not really, nothing special. It's always like that: I know where the machines are and when I pass by them, the urge is stronger than me and it's impossible for me to control myself.

This example clearly illustrates the fact that some gamblers have more difficulty discerning the thoughts that precede a gambling session. Often, they express themselves or act as though they had no control over their decision to gamble and as though the entire thing happened magically. Given that the therapist is well aware that the event did not happen spontaneously and that there were underlying thoughts leading up to gambling, even though the gambler cannot identify them, the therapist continues to interrogate the gambler.

THERAPIST: So, before you gambled, you thought about the machines simply when passing by them.

GAMBLER: Yes. That's right. I was unable to resist.

THERAPIST: When you passed by the machines, what were you thinking about?

GAMBLER: I felt like gambling.

THERAPIST: Okay. So you were near a gambling establishment, you saw the machines and you felt the urge to gamble. All right. It's fairly clear. According to you, why did you gamble? What were you seeking in this activity?

GAMBLER: Well, I was thinking I could win all in one shot. ...

THERAPIST: All in one shot? What do you mean by that?

GAMBLER: I knew that I only had $5 on me, but that I could win. You never know.

THERAPIST: So, you were thinking about the possibility of winning some money?

GAMBLER: Yes. Well, it's already happened to me in the past. Where I won with a small wager, that is.

Although the gambler still believes that nothing preceded the desire to gamble and that he gave in simply because his desire was stronger than him, the therapist's questions have enabled him to understand the thoughts underlying the desire to gamble. Box 3.2 lists six categories of thoughts suggested by Dr. Tony Toneatto, a well-known specialist in the area of excessive gambling. This list can help to highlight certain thoughts, or at the very least function as paths for further questioning.

The examples in Box 3.2 highlight cognitions or erroneous thoughts that are frequently verbalized by the gambler. Other thoughts can be found in the gambling literature. If we grouped the erroneous thoughts entertained by gamblers, we could easily categorize them.

These cognitions or erroneous thoughts are numerous and varied. The first therapy session is crucial with regard to the identification of erroneous thoughts. However, evaluating these erroneous thoughts remains important throughout therapy because the different situations and events experienced by the gambler on a daily basis are susceptible of reinforcing his or her desire to gamble and stimulating new erroneous thoughts that are expressed in later therapy sessions. The identification of erroneous thoughts is highly important because the gambler learns to correct them as they surface.

The daily observation grid

We find it very useful to ask gamblers to complete a daily observation grid throughout the entire therapeutic process. By using this grid, gamblers record a certain amount of information regarding their gambling every day. There are numerous advantages to this task. Given that gamblers tend to underestimate the extent of their gambling problem, this grid helps gamblers to become conscious of their gambling problem, of the intensity of their desire to gamble, and of the substantial sums of money that have been lost. Moreover, the grid enables gamblers to monitor their therapeutic progress. Gamblers can therefore better quantify or objectify the changes taking place throughout therapy. The grid can help gamblers to

Box 3.2   Categories of erroneous thoughts regarding gambling

1. Superstitions
   1.1. Of a cognitive nature: believing that certain mood states or thoughts help the gambler.
   1.2. Of a behavioral nature: believing that certain rituals, practices, or acts have a favorable influence on the gambler's chances of winning.
   1.3. Lucky charm: believing that the possession of a particular object increases the gambler's chances of making significant wins.

2. Selective memory: the memory of past wins is more persistent and more active than that of past losses.

3. Distortion of temporal perception: increasing or decreasing the actual length of time in such a way as to highlight wins and de-emphasize losses. For instance, believing that a series of wins took place in a shorter time span than was actually the case.

4. Overestimating one's abilities: believing to have found the right way of defying or beating the "system".

5. Illusions regarding chance
   5.1 Chance can be controlled: believing that chance can be manipulated in order to control the outcome of the game.
   5.2 Chance is contagious: believing that luck in one area of life announces luck in gambling

6. Interpreting events during a gambling session
   6.1 Attribution: overestimating the power that personal characteristics have on situational variables such as luck.
   6.2 Anthropomorphism: attributing human reactions and characteristics to inanimate objects such as the roulette or slot machines.
   6.3 Error or illusion of control: entertaining an erroneous belief regarding the "laws of average". For instance, believing that a series of losses will inevitably be followed by a win.

realize the extent of their progress when it appears to them that they are no better off after therapy. Finally, this grid provides precious information about the events of the week. Every day, gamblers rate their perception of being in control of their gambling as well as their desire to gamble on a scale from 0 to 100. Gamblers also indicate the frequency with which they gamble by specifying the number of times they gambled during the day, the number of hours spent gambling and the amount of money lost. Lastly, gamblers are asked to write about the feelings they had throughout the day as well as any context or event that may have provoked their urge to gamble. The grid is presented as Figure 3.1 (overleaf).

Conclusion

The evaluation of excessive gamblers involves several dimensions. In addition to assigning a diagnosis based on specific criteria, the therapist must obtain information about the history and evolution of the gambling problem, the particular gambling habits of his or her clients, and their beliefs and thoughts about gambling. The therapist must also evaluate the presence of other problems, such as alcohol or drug dependence, which may interfere with the gambling problem and its treatment. We have also presented evaluation instruments available for assessing gamblers. Although they are not all necessary for the assessment of excessive gamblers, each is useful for various reasons.

Finally, our experience with gamblers has enabled us to observe that evaluating other elements, such as anxiety or depression, is necessary to develop a proper intervention plan. Any other recourse that is deemed useful, such as speaking with the gambler's family and friends, must be taken in order to better understand gamblers who wish to put an end to their destructive gambling habits.

Name: ....

Date:	/ /	/ /	/ /	/ /	/ /	/ /	/ /
1. To what extent do I perceive that my gambling problem is under control? 0 10 20 30 40 50 60 70 80 90 100 not at all a little moderately very much completely							
2. What is my desire to gamble today? 0 10 20 30 40 50 60 70 80 90 100 non-existent weak average high very high							
3. To what extent do I perceive myself as being able to abstain from gambling? 0 10 20 30 40 50 60 70 80 90 100 not at all a little moderately very much completely							
4. Did I gamble today?							
5. How much time (hours and minutes) did I spend gambling?							
6. How much money did I spend on gambling, excluding wins?							
7. Specify your state of mind or the particular events of the day.*							

*By specifying the date, you can write on the back of this page.

Figure 3.1: Daily observation grid

4

THE FUNDAMENTAL PRINCIPLE OF GAMBLING: INDEPENDENCE OF TURNS

Before providing a detailed description of treatment goals for excessive gambling, it is important to be familiar with their underlying principles. Through our experience meeting gamblers and placing them in gaming scenarios, it was possible for us to examine their inner dialogue. Surprisingly, the results of these studies reveal that gamblers' understanding of chance is erroneous. In fact, while they are gambling, 75% of their thoughts are incorrect; that is, they do not adhere to the principle of chance as an unpredictable or uncontrollable event. From this discovery, we proceeded to dissect these erroneous thoughts, thus revealing new information concerning gamblers' sources of motivation.

The motivational sources for gambling are numerous. They include, for example, pleasure or strong sensation seeking, desire to treat oneself to a luxury, escape from unpleasant emotions, need for solitude, desire to beat the "system", and intention of chasing losses. However, by studying gamblers' inner dialogue, we have identified two sources of motivation common to all gamblers: attempting to predict the next win and entertaining a conviction of winning. As the reader will discover, the treatment of excessive gamblers is mainly concerned with these two sources of motivation.

Attempting to predict a win means that gamblers have established clues for themselves that indicate timely moments to go gambling, wager, or increase their bets. Gamblers may say to themselves, for example, that a prayer for a loved one increases their chances of winning and prescribes them to bet right away. Gamblers may also, in their attempts to predict, seek out surefire models or schemas, and meticulously study the game. They may also develop rules of play or strategies in order to control chance. For example, they might believe that low cards in Blackjack announce the arrival of high cards. These errors in thinking, which foster the tendency to predict the game's outcome, have been classified into three categories: non-recognition of independence of turns, illusions of control, and superstitions. These categories and their related errors in thinking will be explained and exemplified below so that the reader may understand both how they are constructed and how they may be challenged.

To better understand what conviction of winning means, imagine the atmosphere of a bus loaded with gamblers on their way to the casino. While on their way, most are excited by the idea of going to a gaming establishment to gamble, while others, in silence, mentally revise strategies that will allow them to outsmart the Roulette or Baccarat table and win. The latter behavior corresponds to what our studies reveal: that gamblers' inner dialogue and mental images before or during a gambling session are generally based on the certainty that the gambling session will unfold in a positive manner and have a happy ending. Gamblers hope and believe they will win. Some may feel invulnerable or all-powerful, possibly qualifying themselves as masters. These gamblers' thoughts reflect their strong tendencies to remember past wins and to mistake their "hope for future wins" for "certainty that they will win".

While there exists a multitude of gambling games, nobody needs to know all their rules and subtleties to understand the mental mechanics of an excessive gambler. Erroneous thoughts concerning their conviction of winning or tendency to predict future wins are more or less the same from one game to another. Though therapeutic examples presented within the current chapter may be true for clients of casinos, bars, or betting parlors, they could just as easily be transposed and exploited according to a gambler's preferred game. In fact, the treatment of gambling is valid for all types of gambling games, and is structured in such a way as to facilitate recognition of erroneous thoughts that contribute to the conviction of winning and the tendency to predict a win.

Until now, the data result from studies of interventions whose goals included complete cessation of gambling. Accepting that gamblers have a strong vulnerability to persist in gambling, stopping gambling represents the main objective of therapy, and is the only one that ensures a favorable outcome.

GAMBLER: Can I still buy simple lottery tickets? Must I stop gambling on all games? I only have a problem with Roulette!

THERAPIST: The treatment that you're undertaking involves the cessation of all games of chance. It is your only guarantee against relapse. To pursue certain gambling activities, even in a controlled manner, constitutes a risky behavior. What would happen if, by misfortune, you win a small sum of money with an inoffensive lottery ticket? Is it possible that this would give you back your taste for Roulette?

It is important to tell gamblers who wish to continue gambling in a controlled fashion – a subject of much controversy among specialized therapists – that it is more prudent to abstain, at least for the duration of treatment. Clarifying this simple requirement helps to prevent gamblers in need of assistance from withdrawing from treatment. However, gamblers must be informed that their view of gambling, like their reaction to giving up this activity, will no longer be the same after treatment. Cognitive therapy, which they are preparing to undertake, will actually allow them to recognize and modify false beliefs that they have adopted concerning gambling, including the idea of mastery, which is the basis of the large majority of relapses. Who knows? Perhaps afterwards the gambler might not want to consider the idea of gambling in a controlled manner.

The principal errors in thinking

Gambling games possess certain characteristics that are likely to foster a private conviction of winning and nourish a tendency to try to predict wins. In this respect, the principal errors in thinking are linked to the excessive gambler's limited knowledge of negative winning expectancy, as well as independence of turns, illusions of control, superstitions, and the fallacious hope of recuperating losses. The various errors in gamblers' thinking are addressed once chance is well defined and understood by gamblers, and once it is no longer confused with skill.

Negative winning expectancy

At a mathematical level, negative winning expectancy corresponds to the sum of money redistributed between gamblers according to the total sum of their bets. In other words, winning expectancy determines what gamblers can expect to gain on the game over a long period of time. The gambling industry must give back less money than they collect in order to make profits. This way of redistributing the money wagered creates a negative winning expectancy that is applicable to all gamblers. With a negative winning expectancy, all that gamblers can expect over the long run are losses.

There exists an interpretative error with regards to the winning expectancy that makes gamblers believe that they have better chances of winning on certain gambling games. Often, they hear that the rate of return is 50, 75, or 92%. Many gamblers make the regrettable error of interpreting these rates as corresponding to the mathematical chances of winning. This interpretation is absolutely false. A return rate of 92% means that gamblers, on a long-term basis, will lose 8% of the money they bet. To speak of return rate is to speak, in a positive way, of a negative winning expectancy.

Negative winning expectancy ensures that the gambling industry makes a large profit when a very large population of gamblers bet, or even when a sole gambler bets repeatedly. The more gamblers bet, and the more the number of their bets increase, the more their chances of losing increase. Winning expectancy varies from one game to another, but it always remains negative. In gambling, gamblers' worst enemy is time since they inevitably lose in the long run.

Thus, if gamblers are subjected to a negative winning expectancy, it is mathematically impossible for gamblers who repetitively bet to recover or recuperate losses. Also, if gambling games are profitable for the gambling industry, they cannot be profitable for the players. All games with a negative winning expectancy are advantageous to the industry.

Most of the time, gamblers claim that they easily understand demonstrations of the negative winning expectancy. Often, they are even aware of this reality. However, inside themselves, they are convinced that they can or will win. In order to help gamblers to integrate the concept of negative winning expectancy, the therapist proposes simple and meaningful examples.

The first example is one of the most eloquent with regards to the impossibility of making up losses by repeatedly betting on gambling games. The scenario involves a betting agent (a "bookmaker" or "bookie") who offers to mediate a Heads or Tails session between two people, while taking in a small commission. Forget about this "mediator" for a short time and imagine that the two people playing, John and Jack, are already playing Heads or Tails and betting. If the coin is tossed only four times, it is possible that Jack will win four consecutive bets and make money. However, if they continue to toss the coin and bet until infinity, John and Jack should expect to obtain heads 50% of the time, and tails the other 50% of the time – in other words, they can expect to win as often as they lose. That means that the game becomes less interesting the more they play because, over a long period of time, nobody wins any money. Thus, making repeated tosses works against the players and cancels their winning expectancy. Figure 4.1 accurately illustrates this no win, no lose situation.

Look, however, at what happens when the bookie begins to toss the coin while demanding an 8% return on the money bet by the players. For each dollar bet, the bookie keeps 8 cents. By not playing very often, John or Jack could come out of this gaming session a winner. For example, out of four tosses, John might fortuitously win four times and quit while ahead. However, John also risks concluding that betting on this game pays and he may continue to bet. Nonetheless, the more they bet, the more time works

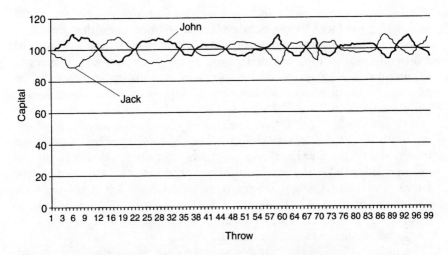

Figure 4.1: The results of tossing a coin between two individuals.

against them. As we saw earlier, the winning and losing turns cancel each other with repeated betting. But in this case, the bookie collects 8% of each bet, which corresponds to a negative winning expectancy. This way, the bookie progressively accumulates, while John and Jack lose over time. This is a statistical and mathematical law. Figure 4.2 shows what happens when two gamblers play Heads or Tails 1,000 times with an 8% negative winning expectancy. True, they occasionally win, but their respective capital ends up decreasing.

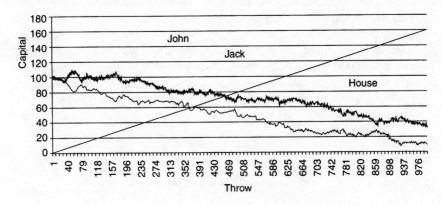

Figure 4.2: The results of tossing a coin between two individuals with a house edge.

As soon as gamblers begin to bet regularly on games of chance, it is impossible for them to get richer: statistics demonstrate that they lose money in the long run. However, they occasionally win small sums of money. Because of these sudden gains, the insidious tendency to want to recuperate their losses, present among many gamblers, is fostered. The paradox lies in the fact that, in order to hope to make up their losses, gamblers have no other choice than to gamble for a long time.

Jennifer has $1,000,000 that she is ready to gamble on video lottery terminals, and all of this money is in her right shirt pocket. How much money should Jennifer have, normally, in her left shirt pocket once she has bet her $1,000,000? If the video lottery terminal has an 8% negative winning expectancy, she will have, more or less, $920,000. If Jennifer then decides to play her $920,000, she will lose another 8%, and so on. By continuing to gamble, Jennifer eventually loses everything and will no longer belong to the millionaire's club.

By definition, excessive gamblers tend to bet repeatedly. In doing so, they lose all of their money, and often that of others. Yet, excessive gamblers are no more unfortunate than other gamblers. They are victims of their determination to play games whose negative winning expectancy leads them nowhere else but to ruin.

Another example might help gamblers to understand what negative winning expectancy means. Challenge them in a game of War. This is a card game for two players in which each player turns over a card at the same time. The player with the highest card wins his or her opponent's card. The goal of the game is to beat one's opponent by taking all the cards.

THERAPIST: As we have just seen, all gambling games have a negative winning expectancy and are created in such a way that the industry is always the winner. Imagine that a bookie challenges you to a game of War. He or she inserts two invincible jokers within his or her own deck of cards and gives you an ordinary deck of cards. It then becomes a game of War where the weapons are unequal. This way of proceeding ensures that you lose in the long run. Obviously, it's possible for you to win a couple of turns if you play few times. However, the more you play, the more you lose since their invincible cards will eventually be played. Repeated turns will lead to you losing.

Independence of turns:
A fundamental concept

One of the principal objectives of therapy is to correct thoughts that ignore the concept of independence of turns. Once gamblers completely understand the independence of turns phenomenon, their conviction of winning and tendency to predict results – which drive them to bet – are seriously shattered or even destroyed. Thus, it is a good strategy to explain this principle at the beginning of therapy, right after having addressed negative winning expectancy, because it is gamblers' natural tendency to make links between events that foster illusions of control and fuel their drive to bet.

The independence of turns phenomenon is very simple to understand, but games of chance are made in such a way as to disguise chance, and gamblers often find themselves trying to defy it. However, the principle of independence of turns applies to all lottery and casino games. Even Blackjack or sports betting cannot escape this phenomenon. So what error in thinking do gamblers commit?

Events are independent of each other when each is considered unique in itself and as having no link with previous or following events. For example, while drinking a coffee, Peter saw a fly land on his shoulder. Then his mother announced that she was going to Cuba to meet a friend. Unless we are superstitious, it is obvious that there is no link between these events. Since they are independent, Peter cannot predict that a fly will land on his shoulder based on the fact that he is drinking a coffee. As for the fly, it does not indicate that Peter is about to learn that his mother is going overseas. In fact, none of these events can help Peter to predict the next event since they are independent of each other.

Independence of turns is the essential condition of games of chance. In order to be unpredictable and to obey the rules of chance, all gambling games are structured in a way that each turn is an independent event that is in no way determined by the results of previous turns. This independence, or absence of a link, necessarily renders useless the observation of results with the goal of predicting the next result. Thus, gamblers can never exert any control over the game.

All human beings spontaneously rely on previous experience and their observations of the present to guide decision making. Thus, gamblers' first reflex is to observe the game in order to discover a constant, to develop a strategy and, consequently, more easily obtain the best result possible. However, gamblers do not seem to suspect that gambling games make observation and strategy useless. The strategies they develop are as futile as the observations they make since each turn is new and previous results in no way allow them to predict the following turn. All attempts to reduce the risk of their bets or to increase their chances of winning are doomed to failure because of the independence of turns. Since the risk of losing is the same at each turn, gamblers cannot evade the negative winning expectancy.

Here is a simple example to help gamblers better grasp what independence of turns in gambling means. The game of Heads or Tails demonstrates that observing previous outcomes of coin tosses is useless when making a new toss. In this example, Mary asks Martina to play Heads or Tails. Mary tosses the coin nine times, and on the tenth toss, she asks Martina to bet on Heads or Tails.

First toss:	**Tails**
Second toss:	Heads
Third toss:	**Tails**
Fourth toss:	**Tails**
Fifth toss:	Heads
Sixth toss:	**Tails**
Seventh toss:	Heads
Eighth toss:	**Tails**
Ninth toss:	**Tails**
Tenth toss:	?

If Martina analyzes the first nine outcomes before betting on the tenth toss, even if for an instant, she is already committing a logical error. Regardless of her reasoning, the chance of heads or tails landing face up is always one out of two, independently of previous tosses. The coin does not remember previous turns and each turn is entirely new. It is thus impossible to increase the accuracy of predictions based on past events or by trying to discover a pattern.

All gambling games are characterized by this essential condition of independence of turns. Aside from variations in the percentages attached to gamblers' winning expectancy, all these games adhere to the same structure. Whether the game is Roulette, horse races, video lottery, Blackjack, or Bingo, these games do not differentiate one bet from another, just like in a series of coin tosses. In all likelihood, the rules and appearance of gambling games are only lures to mask the independence of turns and the unpredictable nature of the game. No game requires observation, intelligence, or skill since each turn is unique and final. Thus, no strategy can be put into place when it comes time to bet. The best way to bet is to put no reliance on any logic or strategy other than obeying the basic rules of the game. In sum, these games never give gamblers the opportunity to bet based on their abilities or their performance. The gambling industry cannot take that risk!

Ignoring or being unaware of independence of turns sometimes pushes gamblers to bet disproportionately. It is common to encounter excessive gamblers who are unrelenting and end up betting more than the expected gain. These gamblers lose sight of the difference between the total sum they bet and the possible winnings. This outrageous betting highlights their idea that the more they gamble, the more they increase their chances of winning. It is easy to understand this determination to bet more than they can possibly win. Since gamblers often lack the means to bet, but believe they are on the brink of winning, they dare not lose any bets. Furthermore, the initial desire to win big is transformed into an imperative need to recuperate lost bets. Gamblers who persist in gambling no longer see that the probability of winning does not increase, even when they string turns together and accumulate losing bets. Their determination to bet indicates that they are not aware that each turn is new.

As mentioned earlier, independence of turns involves the absence of a link between one bet and another. This independence necessarily makes each gambling session as unique as each gambling location. Gamblers who lose Monday, Tuesday, and Wednesday cannot conclude that they will win Thursday. Furthermore, witnessing another gambler's win in no way announces that luck is near or that fortune follows.

Integrating the principle of independence of turns and its practical implications constitutes the gambler's greatest challenge. Understanding that each turn is new consequently negates observation and skill at the game. Moreover, gamblers who recognize this principle realize the absurdity of all the strategies they have employed in order to improve their way of gambling. This realization cannot be accomplished without facing hurdles. While the natural tendency to link events is at the basis of many erroneous thoughts that held gamblers riveted on their favorite game, gamblers who recognize the independence of turns also realize, from then on, that they were wrong the whole time they were gambling, and that this logical error was largely the cause of their excessive gambling. For gamblers, this realization almost corresponds to the crumbling of a dream world.

As therapy progresses, more gamblers accept the idea that gambling games cannot be subjected to logic, skill, or any form of observation for the purposes of prediction. The most naïve of gamblers, if they respect the basic rules of gambling games, have the same chances of winning as the most cunning of gamblers. These games are truly within everybody's reach and it is not without reason that they are so popular. A person needs nothing – neither intelligence nor skill – to participate.

Why can't a person bet on darts, golf, or crosswords in casinos? The reason is simple: the gambling industry systematically eliminates games that offer the possibility of drawing from past events or personal abilities. By only making available games that respect the principle of independence of turns, the industry ensures that no gamblers can acquire experience or improve their abilities. The structure of these games guarantees their peace of mind ... and profits!

It is quite likely that gamblers will continue to believe in the existence of models, patterns, or strategies despite explanations of the independence of turns concept. Gamblers often have a long history and cannot quickly accept that their way of viewing and playing their preferred game goes against the "logic of chance". Their first reflex is to recall past gambling sessions and to convince themselves that their strategies work. From the beginning, gamblers constantly observe the statistics and progress of their favorite game, draw erroneous conclusions, and apply completely useless strategies. Thus, over the course of therapy, gamblers begin to recognize the error of their observations.

Gamblers study the game in a non-systematic manner. Since they hope to win, their expectations lead them to be selective with regards to the information they seek and remember. Their search for high-paying jackpots and their desire to reproduce winning bets leads them to recall preceding events. In order to harmonize their recall of past events with their erroneous perception of the game, they accumulate occasions where their predictions proved to be correct and ignore all the times they were wrong. By ignoring independence of turns, gamblers continue to believe in the predictive value of events.

Based on their observations, gamblers develop strategies that they share with each other. Within the "gambling community", these tricks rise to the rank of myths. For example, gamblers continually find themselves in situations where other gamblers give advice: "You should gamble on this table, the dealer is not lucky today", "Take this machine, it seems to be on a winning streak", etc. All of these remarks shape gamblers' reality and influence their way of thinking. Comforted by erroneous interpretations, gamblers thus have difficulty leaving this world of illusions.

Often, gamblers tenaciously cling to their erroneous ideas: "I know that patterns exist. The problem is that I haven't yet been able to correctly identify them." Sometimes, gamblers have the reflex to reproach themselves for their lack of skill instead of considering the observable nature of chance. This internal attribution of cause allows them to ignore, once more, independence of turns. Again, these erroneous thoughts foster their desire to improve and lead them to observe their preferred game even more.

Certain gambling games, however, employ complex devices and encourage gamblers to observe a sequence. For example, video lottery terminals, with their many images, encourage the observation and search for relationships between turns. Some gamblers even believe that certain images (prunes, oranges, cherries, the number seven, etc.) announce the jackpot. This incorrect belief incites them to continue betting. But, these gamblers forget that they are playing a lottery. Every bet or pressing of the start button is identical: that is, each time they occur, the machine makes a draw for the first time. If gamblers repeatedly bet on the same machine, they are not playing within the context of one big game, but are playing several small and independent games that possess the same probability of winning.

It is very difficult to abandon this reflex to observe everything, including gambling games. Throughout our lifetime, we learn to use past experiences in order to increase mastery over our lives. In this sense, the ability to observe and predict is at the very core of human experience. So, even though the concept of independence of events is easily understood by gamblers during therapy, they quickly forget it as soon as they start gambling again!

Some illustrations favor comprehension of the principle of independence of turns. Thus, when explaining the concrete implications of this condition, which is intrinsic to gambling, the following examples are of valuable assistance. Gamblers who do not know about independence of turns have the distinct propensity to reject lottery tickets that contain a logical suite of numbers (5–10–15–20–25–30) or whose numbers are concentrated (11–13–14–17–18–19). In order to unveil the error in logic behind this choice, one can ask gamblers to imagine that the balls used in the draw are not numbered, but of different colors. Ball 1 becomes a white ball; ball 2, a brown ball; ball 3, a green ball; and so on. With colored balls, it is easier for gamblers to imagine that all ball combinations have the same probability of being drawn. This then means that the combination 1–2–3–4–5–6 (white–brown–green–blue–purple–black) has the same chance of being drawn as the combination 6–15–24–32–41–49 (black–beige–yellow–pink–red–fuchsia).

Thus, independence of turns does not care about numbers, colors … or time! Gamblers who keep the same combination of numbers for several years consider the passing of time as an ally. Such gamblers believe that their combination will either be drawn or that it is impossible for it to not be drawn, which is totally untrue. Since the lottery consists of draws that are completely reset each time, all numbered balls are reinserted into the ball machine for each draw, and the ball machine has no memory of past events. Like all other gambling games, each lottery draw is totally new. Moreover, even if it is unlikely, the same combination could occur several times in succession, while a particular combination may never be drawn.

A pseudo-active lottery (e.g., 6/49) player believed so much in the existence of points of reference that he constructed a mini ball machine and made several draws a day following a precise ritual. Like the majority of gamblers, he was trying to discover combinations of numbers to recreate or avoid. He even established a strategy aiming to improve his predictions. This is an eloquent example of the many useless observations and vain attempts to predict, which are spurred on by lotteries that provide gamblers the opportunity to choose their own numbers.

Gamblers who do not recognize independence of turns maintain the idea that they will soon win, and end up squandering a fortune at the game. The more they gamble, the more they tend to increase their bets since, according to them, the jackpot will soon be paid out. Here are more examples of poor conceptions and false interpretations of the concept of independence of turns, which are largely based on gamblers' certainty of winning:

- "At Roulette, it's better to begin betting when three even numbers have just won. This means that a series of odd numbers will soon occur."
- "At Roulette, I bet on the same number all night. I look at the compilation tables and choose a number that hasn't come out for a long time. After that, I'm faithful to that number!"
- "It's better to ask about how the video lottery terminal's has been behaving over the course of the day. Playing with a machine that has not paid out during the day increases my chances of winning!"
- "At Blackjack, when the dealer is lucky several times in a row, I increase my bet because I'll win soon."

Gamblers might say that it is preferable to change video lottery terminals if it does not pay out after five or six turns. This remark perfectly illustrates how they do not understand the independence of turns phenomenon or the fact that they are playing a lottery. Apparently, gamblers believe that the machine has a register of previous bets made and lots won that it consults in order to choose the opportune moment to pay out another lot. To help gamblers to understand how the programming of video lotteries functions, which is based on random selection, one can provide the following example:

THERAPIST: Imagine that you have twenty scratch-and-win lottery tickets. You scratch five and they're all losing tickets. At that time, would you say that this indicates a trend, and that the rest should be losing tickets?

Gamblers then realize that each ticket has the same probability of being a winning ticket and that tickets that were scratched before do not indicate any trend. Video lotteries work the same way. For each bet or each draw, gamblers either win or lose, regardless of what happened before. Gamblers who take their chances several times in a row on the same terminal actually make several independent draws. Obviously, the more they bet, the more they accumulate losing draws.

The video lottery's trap, as opposed to instant lotteries, is that all the draws happen within the same terminal. Since each bet is not physically separated from the previous one, gamblers become convinced that there is a link between them. They forget that each bet or each trial constitutes a unique and final game in itself. With this type of lottery, it is easy to be mystified into believing that the more one gambles, the more certain it is that the machine will eventually pay out. As a consequence of not understanding the principle of independence of turns, gamblers settle down in front of one machine and do not leave it until they have gambled away all their money. Since gamblers believe that the machine must soon pay out the jackpot, they do not want to leave the machine in any circumstance. Thus, the gambling session can last hours, and even days.

Other gamblers persist in gambling because they believe that they have come close to winning. Contrary to what they believe, nobody comes close to winning. In instant lotteries, for example, the ticket is either winning or losing. A ticket that contains *almost* all the digits required to take home a prize of $50,000 is nothing but a losing ticket. Thus, if the number 17 is drawn in the lottery, and a gambler unfortunately bet on 18, he or she did not come close to winning. With chance, we win or we lose, but we never come close to anything. Just as in pregnancy, either a woman is or is not; she cannot be just a little pregnant! Also, we do not come close to speaking to a friend if, when dialing their phone number, we invert the last two numbers.

Another example can be presented to gamblers to help them to understand what independence of turns means. For this example, gamblers are asked to consider a ball machine within which there is one sole red ball among 1,000 white balls. Gamblers imagine that they are betting on their chances of drawing the red ball with their eyes covered. If, in their mind, they draw a white ball, we ask them to put the ball back and to bet again. Are gamblers closer to drawing the red ball after 300 consecutive draws? Since the game resets after each draw, gamblers understand that each time they draw, they only have one out of 1,000 chances of winning; even after betting 300 times, their chances of drawing the red ball remain the same. Moreover, while playing video lotteries, gamblers often vary the speed of their bets. This example concerning the red ball helps them to realize that making 300 rapid or slow draws does not change their chances of drawing the red ball.

GAMBLER: I would like to believe that each turn is new. However, according to the law of averages, when I play a video lottery terminal, it has to pay out money after a while!

THERAPIST: A video lottery terminal has no will and it's not playing with you. Each time you bet, you make a draw that is independent of others and that, by way of chance, determines whether you'll win or not. Each time that you push the start button, it's as if you're drawing a winning or losing lot. The programming for this lottery game produces millions of winning and losing combinations during the same day, it is possible you could draw only non-paying combinations. Furthermore, there is no way of knowing when to press the start button in order to win. In this type of lottery, since it is a lottery, gamblers make several blind draws. When gambling on this type of game, the chances of winning are reset with each draw.

GAMBLER: Yes, but what happens with full machines? For example, when a gambler loses 1,000 dollars in the same machine, it has no choice but to give some of the money back!

THERAPIST: Whether the machines are full or empty does not influence the random nature of the lottery's number generator. The electronic aspect of the computer is not linked to the more mechanical aspect where money is involved. Whether there are 15,000 dollars or $10 in the machine does not change the chances of winning or losing. Each time you gamble, your chances are reset, like when you try to draw a red ball among 1,000 white balls.

Because it is particularly eloquent, this last example is a good one to present to gamblers who continue to believe that they cannot always lose and that they will end up winning money by gambling. Nothing allows them to draw this conclusion since each turn is entirely new. Gamblers can continually lose. As long as gamblers think that the turns are dependent upon one another, they are tricked by the attraction of strategies or prediction systems. Conversely, gamblers who correctly integrate the principle of independence of turns are freed of numerous erroneous thoughts. It is thus important that gamblers master this fundamental principle of chance.

Illusions of control

The majority of excessive gamblers believe they accumulate experience and learn from their errors when gambling. In truth, this feeling of personal efficacy is a considerable handicap and gamblers who believe that their actions influence their chances of winning are victims: they maintain the illusion that they will beat the industry by defying the negative winning expectancy and by recuperating their monetary losses. Those gamblers are beset by illusions of control – mirages of the mind that reinforce their motivation to continue gambling.

By gambling, gamblers naturally attempt to discover a way of accessing the jackpot. In pursuing this objective, they integrate elements of logic, superstition, observation, or calculation. They quickly develop personal strategies, adopt ritualized behavior, imagine tricks, or create systems in order to increase their chances of winning. Gamblers who believe in the use of strategies only maintain, in fact, illusory thoughts since there is nothing that will allow them to overcome the obstacle of independence of turns. Since strategy or mastery of the game has no relationship with chance, these kinds of activities reflect an "illusion of control". Memorizing Blackjack cards, studying statistics concerning the Roulette marble, or choosing anniversary dates for the lottery are examples of behaviors whose purpose is to foresee the unpredictable.

As gambling activities are not games of skill, no mental or physical skills are necessary when it comes to betting. However, the majority of gamblers are convinced that it is possible for them to acquire some form of mastery in order to solve the enigma posed by these games. Each gambler thus develops personal strategies and those who win are hailed as masters. Games of chance are falsely transformed into games of skill and gamblers are more and more deceived about the nature of the gambling activity. It is obvious that chance occasionally favors gamblers; but, regardless of the strategies used, the wins they pocket are based on nothing but chance.

However, gaming sessions are rich in coincidences that reinforce the idea of mastery in gamblers' minds. Pure coincidences between behaviors and prizes won eventually convince them that certain chance events are not chance. The more they play, the more they adopt the false belief that their behavior has a real impact on the lots they win. Furthermore, they are rewarded with a sense of personal pride when they win and, conversely, feel profound shame when they lose. Curiously, repeated disappointments do not manage to destroy their illusions of mastery. In fact, they accentuate them.

Financially, when it comes time to bet, gamblers only need the financial capacity to risk capital and lose it over time. However, the cognitive universe of the gambler is much more complex than the apparently banal game lets on. In fact, there most certainly exist as many illusions of control as there are individuals who gamble. In order to provide an overview of this matter, the following pages provide accounts of illusions of control, which have been conjured up by gamblers and that are associated with the most popular games of chance.

Lotteries
At the present time, there are several kinds of lotteries on the market and it may be difficult to make sense of them. Let us just say here that the bulk of

lotteries are either passive lotteries where gamblers do not choose the numbers, instant lotteries or "scratch and wins", and the Lotto (pseudo-active lotteries) where gamblers select a series of numbers or sports teams. In their apparently innocuous forms, lotteries open the door to multiple illusions of control. At this game, it is illusory for gamblers to think they can defy chance:

- by choosing anniversary dates as numbers;
- by keeping statistics on the winning numbers of previous draws;
- by keeping the same combination of numbers from one draw to another;
- by betting on favorite or lucky numbers;
- by avoiding patterns of numbers on the lottery form or ticket;
- by buying their tickets from different locations:
- by studying the statistics and development of sports teams, etc.

Bingo
Bingo is a simple game. A numbered ball is drawn from a large ball machine and gamblers who possess the same number on their card mark it. The player wins a prize if the numbers marked on their card form, for example, a horizontal, vertical, or diagonal line. At this game, it is illusory for gamblers to think they can defy chance:

- by choosing cards that contain their favorite numbers;
- by marking the numbers on their card in a certain manner;
- by choosing a table where nobody has won for a long time;
- by avoiding cards that contain numbers they do not like;
- by going to play with a person that they consider to be lucky, etc.

Video lotteries
Video lottery terminals generally present a visual aspect suitable to engendering strong illusions of control. Video terminals offer a large number of games. While they all function similarly electronically, these gambling games assume several faces: games with fruit, bells, or pots of gold are most notably found, as are cards or electronic *keno*.

Video lottery games make up a fertile terrain for illusions of control. Nevertheless, as its name indicates, video lottery is nothing more than a lottery. This means that gamblers are making a draw the moment they press the start mechanism. At that instant, even before the images are activated, the outcome is already determined. Thus, it is useless to use the stop button in order to catch a winning combination. Moreover, the sole function of selecting the cards, numbers, lines, or series on which to bet is to amuse the player. Gamblers can never apply strategies that provide information about when and where to bet in order to increase their chances of winning. All gamblers' actions are pointless and can in no way influence the machine's programming. Only the amount bet will make the size of the potential prize vary. The application of strategies in no way modifies the probabilities of winning. Overall, for video lotteries, gamblers' behavior and choices are not important, neither is the type of game, nor is the number of draws. Each time they bet, they come up against the same probability of winning. At this game, it is illusory for gamblers to think they can defy chance:

- by discovering winning or losing patterns or cycles;
- by stopping the symbols themselves after having activated the machine's start button;
- by choosing their machine according to the gains that it procured over the course of the day, as if there were full machines or empty machines;
- by choosing a video lottery terminal on which another player has just bet a lot of money;
- by testing the video lottery terminal with small initial bets;
- by playing at precise times or with a particular machine;
- by varying the stakes or switching to another machine;
- by abandoning the machine for a moment or changing the game;
- by pressing the start button in different ways (by varying the force, by creating a routine, by varying the rhythm of the bets, etc.);
- by betting a larger sum when they have just made an appreciable win;
- by returning to gamble at opening time when they lost the evening before;
- by calculating in their head the number of bets they made, the time they spent on the machine, etc.

Blackjack
Blackjack is a card game whose basic rules are simple. A certain number of gamblers play simultaneously, and the goal of the game is to accumulate cards that make up a better total than the dealer, without going over 21. Gamblers automatically win against the dealer if they obtain 21 in only two cards, which is considered to be a Blackjack. Since this is a game of cards where gamblers bet against an opponent – the dealer – Blackjack amateurs are convinced that their skills will be severely tested. Thus, they quickly develop complex game styles and strong illusions of control. They believe that Blackjack requires particular strategies and, as a general rule, they detest being compared to Bingo players, believing that Blackjack is a noble game and cannot be played by just anybody.

But Blackjack is not different from other games of chance. It, too, offers gamblers a negative winning expectancy. Moreover, there are no strategies that are worth being identified here. However, the complexity of the strategies proposed by certain popular books, as well as the probability tables associated with each strategy, are enough to convince Blackjack fanatics that it is indeed a game of skill. Yet, perhaps unfairly, gamblers only slightly minimize their losses when playing the best way possible, but will never gratify their hope of getting richer in the long run. At this game, it is illusory for gamblers to think they can defy chance:

- by memorizing and counting cards;
- by choosing a particular table, location, or dealer;
- by observing the cards dealt to other players in order to determine if they should request another card;
- by observing the playing style of other gamblers before beginning to play;
- by slowing down or speeding up the game's rhythm;
- by making very high bets.

Roulette

Roulette is also a very straightforward game. In this game, gamblers bet on a number on which they think a marble, tossed onto a rotating circular plate, will land. While this game can be compared to a draw wherein chances of winning are reset each time, its visual devices and its numerous betting options disguise chance and create the illusion of a game of skill. The numbers are displayed in apparent disorder within a circular plate, inciting gamblers to uncover the game's mystery. Moreover, human intervention, as manifested by the tossing of the ball, leads gamblers to observe the croupier's gestures, behavior, and even style, such as his or her way of tossing the marble, with the purpose of developing the best prediction system possible. At this game, it is illusory for gamblers to think they can defy chance:

- by observing the way the croupier tosses the marble (force, rhythm, regularity, and consistency);
- by choosing a particular table, location, or croupier;
- by observing previous tosses and creating a statistics sheet;
- by betting on favorite or lucky numbers;
- by observing a player who wins and following that person's betting style;
- by increasing the bets when the marble lands near one of their preferred numbers.

Horse race betting

Horse races also convince gamblers of their ability to predict results. The trap is flagrant. Gamblers must bet on the horses that will cross the finish line first. For their "information", guides containing statistical analyses are made available to them. Again here, it is easy to confuse chance and skill, and to attempt to make the most of one's intelligence or experience when it comes time to bet.

However, one study demonstrates that horse race regulars obtain the same return as beginners: all things considered, they lose as much. Certain bettors qualify themselves as horse race specialists, even if their financial situation is a veritable disaster. These gamblers fully maintain the illusion of being able to predict the results of races to come, as if chance is subject to a logical and predictive science. They are persuaded that their skills can only improve and that experience works to their advantage. Many "specialists" of horse races toy with the dream of making a living from their "science". At this game, it is illusory for gamblers to believe they can defy chance:

- by studying the horses' performance statistics;
- by measuring the speed of their favorite horses;
- by relying on the rebound phenomenon, that is when a horse whose result was poor on its last race does better on the following race;
- by considering the distance or the type (grass or hard-packed dirt) of race track;
- by analyzing the horses' physical characteristics (gait, bearing, muscle tone, etc.).

Shedding their illusions

Rarely do gamblers object to the idea of illusion of control. They even understand it easily. But, when they leave the therapist's office or the therapy room, and they remember the experiences of past games, dissonance resonates through them. Happily, the therapist will have strategically warned them that this dissonance might happen and that it is merely a sign of change. Along the same lines, all gamblers' objections are important, in that they allow for the discovery of other illusory thoughts. As long as gamblers speak of game strategies and mastery, they are demonstrating that they do not understand the implications of independence of turns. For this reason, it is important to frequently review this principle.

In order to free themselves from their destructive passion for gambling, gamblers must not only combat their own illusions, but also those that are suggested to them. Since the gambling market is extremely profitable, the industry benefits by taking advantage of gamblers' illusions. Studies reveal that the more gamblers actively participate in a gambling game, the more they fall prey to illusions of control. The majority of games found on the market are conceived and fabricated in such a way that gamblers confuse them with games of skill. It is not surprising that current games of chance offer an abundance of choices. Certain video lottery games invite gamblers to stop the images rolling before them, even if this action is totally pointless. Such possibilities translate into an intention to mask chance and to let gamblers believe that they affect the outcome of the game. Aside from the deceptive function of these choices, they can be perceived as challenges that are worth mastering. The main purpose of choices in gambling games is to reinforce the gambler's propensity to attempt to master chance.

The gambling industry constantly renews the appearance of games that are put on the market, while in fact, the industry is only perfecting traps that give rise to illusions of control. Thus, the appearances of games are frequently modified and gamblers find themselves before illusory effects that are as impressive as they are efficacious. Nowadays, electronic game specialists, with their science, strive to create new interactive video lottery games and instant lotteries on CD ROM for which interaction is useless. Disguised as games of skill, these new video games continue to be subject to the laws of chance – an important detail that escapes gamblers only too often.

Thus, illusions of control, which appear to be a natural reflex for gamblers, are generally reinforced by a game's appearance. These illusions of mastery over the game are even taken advantage of and exploited in certain non-scientific books that address methods of winning at gambling games. These books only spread false ideas by encouraging gamblers to count on their skills. Even if illusions of control sometimes appear to be of a knowledgeable character, they are often based on ludicrous suggestions or magical perceptions. Superstitions count among these disconcerting ideas that give gamblers the impression that they are increasing their power over the game.

Superstitions

Superstitions, which constitute a category of illusions of control, are innumerable. Whether they are expressed as thoughts or by actions, the function of superstitions is to elude chance. Thus, they often go hand in hand with excessive gambling behavior. Through superstitious thinking, gamblers increase their natural conviction of winning tenfold and believe they are improving their ability to predict wins. Because of their ritualized, magical, or sacred nature, these thoughts partly determine the behavior of those who entertain them. However, since they often defy logic, gamblers are reluctant to say them out loud. Some will even try to camouflage their superstitions and act as though they do not adhere to any. In this case, the therapist's task is to identify them.

There are notably two strategies that bring gamblers to reveal their superstitious thoughts. Speaking openly of a superstition and asking gamblers whether they ever entertain this type of idea is the first option. The second calls for the rehabilitation of superstitions by recognizing gamblers' propensities to have such thoughts by naming a few. These two tactics encourage the expression of thoughts that defy logic. Gamblers' irrational attachment to certain superstitions can sometimes leave the observer completely perplexed.

- "The 21st is a lucky day since it's composed of the number 7 three times."
- "I often win right after having eaten a sandwich. True, it sounds bizarre, but it works."
- "When I don't try to win, I win. My desire to win makes me lose. I must learn to play for pleasure."
- "I gamble with my deceased father's watch. It guides me."

Highlighting the connection between excessive gambling behavior and this type of thinking is something that will be worked on in therapy. In certain cases, superstitions may be shaken through basic questioning whose purpose is to test gamblers' "reality". For example, the therapist might ask gamblers if they have ever lost even if, beforehand, they felt a premonition to the contrary. Along the same lines, they might verify whether gamblers have won in the absence of such a presentiment.

Certain gamblers easily part with their superstitions and react very well when they are asked to question themselves concerning the reliability of their predictions. However, since it is a question of irrationality, logical arguments may lead in the wrong direction, provoking a hardening in gamblers and reinforcing their erroneous perceptions. Superstitious gamblers possess personal thought systems. Given that their superstitious beliefs ensure their psychological balance, gamblers cannot completely ignore them. It is thus better to employ other methods when dealing with this type of gambler and when thoughts of this nature must be addressed.

Is it possible that gamblers confound real life with games of chance? Is it possible that they wrongly believe that their intuition could be used to their advantage in games whose long-term results are determined beforehand? In this way, gamblers are induced to understand that they are committing an error and are not stupid to have superstitious thoughts. Thus, they find themselves free to maintain this belief in other realms of their life and their thought structure is saved. After all, who are we to pretend that there are no situations in which intuitive thoughts pay dividends?

Hope of recuperating losses

Superstitious ideas resurface throughout therapy and it is important to remain aware of them for many reasons, including the fact that they encourage the hope of winning back money that was lost. Certain specialists and therapists are of the opinion that the hope of winning back losses constitutes the principal source of motivation for excessive gamblers. This opinion is risky in that the therapist may attempt to convince gamblers that they are gambling to win. Such an approach has the effect of dissuading gamblers who do not recognize themselves within this hypothesis and, without a doubt, curb their collaboration. In fact, the lure of wins as the most important source of motivation appears somewhat simplistic, given the multiple sources of motivation for gambling. Admittedly, the objective pursued by people who play these games is to make money quickly. However, for some gamblers, the lure of a win may be only an external representation of other underlying sources of motivation.

Nonetheless, even if it remains silent, the hope of recuperating losses is very damaging for the majority of gamblers and it figures among the principal erroneous ideas. With time, the gambling fanatic becomes prisoner of the present and clings to the possibility of soon winning: "Yes, but ... tonight, I can win." By ignoring probabilities and taking refuge in the possibility of imminent gain, gamblers find a basis for their reasoning and perpetuate the gambling cycle. For each problem they suffer, gambling is, repeatedly, the only short-term solution. Their pressing need to win prevents them from considering past losses or to view things within a long-term perspective. Since a rapid gain has already helped them to avoid financial ruin, gamblers see only this unique solution for all their troubles.

The hope of recuperating losses exerts its power for a long time. Accordingly, as gamblers hope to win in the present, they are invited to ask themselves about the possible consequences related to quickly winning a sum of money by gambling. If they are honest in their attempt to give up gambling, gamblers will recognize that a win leads to worse consequences than just losing their bets. Winning immediately reinforces the idea that they have mastered the game, reviving their hope of recuperating lost money, and maintaining their conviction of winning.

It is very difficult to free oneself from the hope of recuperating losses: expecting a rapid win is even more attractive since gamblers have previously known happy outcomes. They clearly remember the sudden feelings of joy associated with important gains and, generally, poorly remember the dejection that seized them at the time of grave losses. Thus, gambling sessions are well imprinted upon their minds and they easily resurface within their memories. Conversely, while painful, losses are often forgotten. So, obsessed by memories of gains, gamblers convince themselves that if they are even a little lucky, they will eventually win. Many gamblers foster the illusion that it is possible to win back losses by gambling and, paradoxically, repeat losses do not manage to decrease this desire. In fact, few gamblers know the total amount of their losses.

Here is an amusing and very revealing analogy. The *slinky* is a flexible spring that is sold as a toy for children. It can slide from one hand to the other or go down stairs (see Figure 4.3). This simple toy illustrates the risks associated with the temptation to make an immediate gain and helps gamblers to understand the consequences of gambling in the long run. Furthermore, it helps them to consider all their losses objectively and shows them where excessive gambling leads to.

THERAPIST: Let's consider the image of a *slinky* going down a set of stairs. The *slinky* always recoils a little in order to better go down the staircase. Have you ever seen *slinky* go up stairs?

A small prize obtained through gambling may be considered as encouragement to continue betting. In fact, these are lures that only nourish the hope of recuperating losses. Certain specialists call this intermittent reinforcement. With the slinky example, one sole step of the staircase is isolated to help gamblers to understand that the hope of winning in the short run always has the same result in the long run, regardless of whether they are at the top or the bottom of the stairs. Each time they gamble, gamblers only consider the possibility of winning, and lose sight of all their losses. At each step, the same scenario inevitably repeats itself and the urgency of the present acts on gamblers like blinders. Each time they

Figure 4.3: A *slinky* illustrating how immediate gains are related, in the long run, to the accumulation of significant losses.

hope to make a rapid gain, gamblers forget that they are on the staircase; that is, on the path of losses. This example demonstrates that it is absurd for gamblers to think they are only present at the time of wins and absent for losses. The mathematical structure of these games is inescapable: in the long run, gamblers eventually go down the staircase.

It is to the gambler's advantage to cease hoping to recuperate losses through gambling. He or she has the ability to stop the *slinky*'s descent by completely ceasing to play. Giving up gambling, however, involves rejecting the idea of being able to play in a controlled manner or being able to leave a gambling session at an opportune moment.

It is in the interest of gamblers, whose objective is to abstain from gambling, to accept the fact that their passion makes them different from the occasional gambler. This acceptance is progressive since many gamblers harbor a profound desire or wish to be able to gamble in a controlled or moderated manner, as if such control would prove that they were normal or like other gamblers. Thus, it is not surprising that gamblers believe they can control themselves and that this sole belief can lead to relapse. Gamblers who let themselves be fooled by the idea that they can stop gambling when they wish and keep to a predetermined sum of money, inevitably fit into at least one of the following molds:

- If they gamble and win, they think they can reproduce this gain or they want to win more money. They continue to gamble and end up losing.
- If they gamble, win and are able to leave with their winnings, they tell themselves that gambling is a good way of obtaining money quickly. They return to play and eventually lose.
- If they gamble, win, play their winnings, and lose them, they tell themselves that the next time they will stop gambling in time. They return to play and inevitably lose again.
- If they gamble and lose, they then want to recuperate the money they lost. They think only of their wins. They persist in playing, and lose.
- If they gamble and lose, they tell themselves that the next time will be better. They return to play and eventually lose.

Once gamblers are aware of their errors in thinking regarding gambling, they know that they can only expect negative consequences in the long run, regardless of a particular gambling session's outcome. The excessive gambler, whether he or she wins or loses, is always a loser.

5

TREATMENT OF THE EXCESSIVE GAMBLER: THE COGNITIVE APPROACH

In this chapter, gamblers will find information that will help them to understand what incites them to gamble, sometimes frenetically; they can learn from this information and complete certain exercises that will assist them to achieve their goal of abstention from gambling. Family members or friends will discover why they are not responsible for their loved one's excessive gambling, or how their brother, spouse, or friend has fallen into the vicious cycle of excessive gambling. Therapists or resource people can easily integrate this new information, not as techniques or recipes to be rigidly followed, but as targets for intervention. These are accompanied by numerous examples from our clinical experience that are presented in the form of excerpts from various therapy sessions between excessive gamblers and therapists.

In order to provide an overview of treatment that is specific to excessive gambling, we will briefly outline the intervention targets that make up the pillars of the bridge leading to the cessation of gambling. Then, each of these targets will be re-examined in more detail with examples. In our opinion, excessive gamblers attain success when they are able to experience the urge to gamble, all the while knowing why they refuse to give in to it once more.

Intervention targets: an overview

For excessive gambling, observing the problem is the most important step in the majority of treatments. Thus, during assessment, we induce gamblers to express the thoughts that crossed their minds before, during, and after a recent gambling session. What we call observation of a gaming session is a pivotal step in treatment, since gamblers have the occasion to express all the ideas that incite them to gamble and that keep them captivated by gambling activities. For example, we ask them about their thoughts concerning their ability to outsmart chance; we examine the extent to which they feel the conviction of winning. Observation of a gambling session is also used to discover whether gamblers attempt to use strategies in order to win the game, whether they entertain any superstitions, or whether they attribute credibility to premonitions. Overall, we want gamblers to speak to us about their personal way of approaching gambling games, without challenging their ideas or behaviors.

Observation of a gambling session can reveal the thoughts that make gamblers vulnerable to gambling. To the extent that a gambler entertains false ideas concerning his or her chances of winning or ability to thwart the "system", it can be said to the same extent that he or she possesses erroneous beliefs. The treatment gamblers are preparing to undergo will attack these particular types of ideas. Being well aware of gamblers' erroneous ideas thus constitutes the first step in this treatment.

Once gamblers' erroneous beliefs are known, they are asked to represent the place that gambling takes up in their life by coloring in the corresponding proportion of a circle. This exercise allows the gamblers to discuss the intrusive character of gambling, while giving them the possibility of expressing certain feelings that only they experience. Gamblers then have the chance to question themselves about their real motivation for ceasing to gamble. Their ambivalence with regards to giving up gambling is examined and they write down their thoughts on this subject. This exercise can be used as a memory aid that gamblers can reread when their desire to gamble is intense.

We teach gamblers to be wary of the many events that are likely to shake their motivation to quit and provoke a relapse. The gamblers thus identify as many situations as they can that might incite their urge to gamble. They can, for example, mention that receiving a bill is a situation that could lead them to relapse. At this step, we ask gamblers to develop personal strategies to circumvent the risk associated with such situations.

Because this is a treatment specific to games of chance, it is important that gamblers be able to provide an accurate definition of the word "chance". All excessive gamblers have an erroneous understanding of chance, which fosters their taste for gambling; and it is for this reason that it is important to clarify the term. The definition of chance is central to therapy because gamblers will refer to it many times over the course of subsequent therapy sessions. Actually, the more the gambler masters the concept of chance and is able to make the distinction between games of skill and games of chance, the more he or she is likely to be freed from the illusions created by gambling games.

Often, excessive gamblers forget the real meaning of the word "chance" once they get the urge to gamble. A disastrous life situation, intense emotions, and favorite games form a screen that prevents them from realizing that they are about to deal with chance. Each time, a return to gambling takes on the form of a combat between sides with unequal weapons. Gamblers allow themselves be deceived by the illusions and, moreover, they do not realize the traps that games of chance conceal. Thus, they are unable to resist them. For example, gambling games are disguised to make gamblers believe that it is possible to predict a win. Gamblers, who seek the best way to win the jackpot, essentially bet on the idea that they can, one day, master the game. Accordingly, gamblers develop a string of erroneous ideas regarding these games. Our task consists of creating some doubt as to the veracity of these beliefs. At this stage, the intervention target is to bring gamblers to recognize the erroneous beliefs that occupy their minds. At this point in therapy, we present information concerning the monetary return of different games of chance, independence of turns, illusions of control, superstitions, the desire to win back lost money, etc. Furthermore, as therapy progresses, gamblers succeed in replacing their erroneous ideas with correct and appropriate thoughts, thus assisting them in attaining their goal of abstinence from gambling.

The exercises, whose purpose is to modify thinking, make up the core of treatment and aim to make gamblers aware of their gambling behavior. Furthermore, the majority of therapy sessions gravitate around these exercises. By repeating each exercise, gamblers learn to control the thoughts that incite them to gamble, thus helping them to shed the illusory hope of recuperating losses.

Gamblers who apply the techniques needed for modifying erroneous thoughts considerably increase their chances of giving up gambling. However, as there are no miracle treatments as yet, the issue of relapse risk is addressed and gamblers examine the different scenarios that are likely to make them act again on their urge to gamble. Finally, the cessation of therapy is gradual in order to maintain therapeutic gains. Therapy terminates when gamblers master the technique of cognitive modification and are fully aware of the risks of relapse.

The course of therapy is simple. At the beginning of each session, the therapist collects the self-observation form presented within a preceding chapter and asks about the client's gambling behavior. A brief review of the concepts outlined previously is conducted and the therapist examines the exercises that he or she has completed over the previous days. During the meeting, new treatment issues and elements are presented, which are followed by a discussion concerning the application of these issues and elements. At the end of the therapy session, gamblers are told what exercises to complete during the following week. Here are the therapeutic targets in detail.

Observation of a gambling session

Observation of a gambling session reveals the erroneous thoughts that gamblers entertain before, during, and after a recent gambling session. The more that is known about gamblers' erroneous thoughts, the more they can be helped to question them when the related exercises have been completed. The gambler's last gambling session is an easy one to observe since it is, most of the time, still fresh in his or her mind. The therapist attempts to uncover the context, situation, or element that created the gambler's desire to gamble, as well as the thoughts that led to his or her acting upon this urge. During this retrospective account, the therapist attempts to discover the gambler's erroneous thoughts related to the conviction of winning and the tendency to predict wins. Furthermore, at this stage, the therapist works at getting clients to speak without restraint. Accordingly, a non-judgmental curiosity regarding the gambler's erroneous thoughts is, without a doubt, the best way to obtain his or her collaboration.

In order to facilitate the discovery of erroneous ideas, gamblers imagine their last gambling session and the therapist questions them about it, starting with what gave them the desire to gamble. Gamblers then reconstruct the inner dialogue that transpired from the moment the first thought related to gambling was triggered to the moment when they returned home from their gambling session. For example, a gambler may recall what he told himself when he unexpectedly received a certain sum of money. Did he say to himself that this sum would allow him to bet only twenty dollars and that he would be able to keep to this amount? Did he say to himself that it wouldn't be so bad if he lost the money since he was not expecting it? Here, the ways of perceiving the initial event are limitless, but they already provide some indication of the way the gambler thinks. Then, what does the gambler do, what does the gambler say, and why?

The therapist systematically asks questions about all of the gambler's actions and all the thoughts he had. How does he choose where he gambles and why does he choose that place over another? Does the gambler have a preferred location or a favorite game? Does he have favorite numbers, certain habits, or a particular ritual when he gambles? Does he have a personal way of betting? Does he use any strategies? If so, what are they? How does he determine whether he will increase, decrease, or maintain his bets? Does he have any clues that indicate when to bet? Does he believe he can recuperate his losses? Does he think he will eventually be able to outplay the game? After having won or lost a sum of money, what does he tell himself? Does the gambler keep statistics on past gambling sessions? Over the course of the therapist's search for erroneous thoughts, he or she assesses to what extent the gambler is confident of winning and at what point this confidence appears. Is he confident from the moment the initial event that leads him to gamble appears? Does it manifest itself over the course of the gambling session? Moreover, does the gambler attribute certain credibility to intuitions or have any superstitions? The therapist notes the responses to these questions and will address them at a later stage.

Since this first part of treatment becomes the foundation for subsequent sessions, we would like to provide a detailed account of a therapist's examination of a gambling session by reproducing a discussion between a therapist and a gambler:

THERAPIST: You told me that you gambled last night. Could you tell me what made you want to gamble?

GAMBLER: There's nothing special to tell. I gambled and I lost 420 dollars. This is so frustrating! I think we should abolish these games!

THERAPIST: And before going gambling, were you frustrated?

GAMBLER: I wasn't at all frustrated. I would even say that I was feeling good. I was at home, relaxing and watching television. There was nothing in particular going on.

THERAPIST: You were relaxing, and it was at this moment that your desire to gamble came about?

GAMBLER: I remember that my wife asked me what I wanted to do for Christmas vacation. At that moment, I was scared because I had spent all the money that was to be used for that holiday. So I avoided the subject on the pretext of needing to get some air. You know, my wife knows that I'm getting treatment, but she doesn't know that I continue to gamble.

Given that the purpose of verbalizing a recent gambling session is to discover the gambler's erroneous ideas about the game, the therapist is not distracted by this new element concerning the lie the gambler made to his wife. By doing so, the therapist ensures that the gambler's discourse does not become tangential and that the objective of the exercise is not lost. The therapist thus sticks to getting the gambler to describe the context, situation, or element that generates this desire to gamble, and to reveal the erroneous thoughts occurring at the time when the gambler made the decision to gamble.

THERAPIST: Thus, it was when you went for a walk that the desire to gamble came to you?

GAMBLER: I would say yes. I wanted to escape my problems. It often happens that way.

THERAPIST: Do you remember saying something to yourself at that moment?

At this point, the therapist attempts to reach into the gambler's inner dialogue, to discover the thoughts that are at the origin of the decision to gamble.

GAMBLER: No, I wasn't thinking about anything. I wanted to escape my problems. Roulette doesn't criticize me and it allows me to clear things up. I don't owe it anything. It all happens between me and Roulette.

THERAPIST: If I understand you right, at that moment, you were thinking that the game would help you to clear things up?

GAMBLER: As soon as I touch the Roulette table, I calm down and become myself. It's all of a sudden. Just like that.

THERAPIST: On your way to the casino, what were your thoughts?

GAMBLER: I was telling myself that my wife deserves better and that I can't always lose.

THERAPIST: How did you feel at that moment?

GAMBLER: I was already seeing myself offering a trip down south to my wife. I was keyed up and this feeling was inspiring me.

THERAPIST: What did this keyed up feeling inspire in you?

GAMBLER: Since I had just lost a couple of times, I told myself that I was on the brink of winning. I don't know why, but most of the time, when my wife wants something, I win.

In these last lines, the gambler's conviction of winning was easy to identify. However, sometimes a gambler's discourse does not describe the lure of a win as easily. In this case, we can be tempted to make gamblers see that they gamble to win. But, by confronting gamblers in that way, there is a risk that they will revolt or will simply not recognize their intention to win. Thus, there are no advantages to adopting such a strategy. Focusing on the detection of erroneous thoughts that manifest over the course of a gambling session allows the therapist to avoid this trap. This process, which consists of reconstructing the gambling situation in order to explore it, is very efficacious because the gambler can easily imagine being in that situation. Accordingly, the gambler is able to express erroneous thoughts that occur within this context more clearly.

THERAPIST: At the beginning of the interview, you told me that you're like all gamblers. However, I would like you to speak about your own personal way of playing Roulette. In fact, I'm more interested in knowing about *your* gambling style. Once you got to the casino, how did you decide which Roulette table you should play?

This last question gives the gambler the possibility of either verbalizing the ideas he uses to predict wins or those that let him remain confident about the existence of winning strategies. Once the gambler is engaged in one or the other strings of thought, the therapist does not hesitate to question the motivation that incites each action or gambling behavior. Since all these actions and behaviors associated with gambling are likely to disguise erroneous thoughts, the therapist continues along these lines until all these ideas are revealed.

GAMBLER: I didn't choose just any Roulette table. First of all, I observed the croupiers. I hate croupiers that toss the marble in any which way. So I chose a croupier with a consistent toss.

THERAPIST: What do you mean by a consistent toss?

GAMBLER: I only play with a croupier that always tosses the marble with the same force.

THERAPIST: Why?

GAMBLER: Since I always play the same numbers, I watch the board for the numbers that have been previously drawn. If the numbers are close to those that I usually choose, then I start to bet on that table. However, if the croupier tosses the marble with an unequal force turn after turn, it doesn't help me.

THERAPIST: I understand. And why do you always gamble with the same numbers?

GAMBLER: Those are my lucky numbers.

THERAPIST: How's that?

During the observation of a gambling session, all of the gambler's assertions are closely scrutinized. Thus, following a gambler's comment, the therapist often asks more than one question in order to make sure no erroneous thoughts escaped his or her grasp, since each erroneous thought is likely to be supported by other erroneous thoughts.

GAMBLER: No reason.

THERAPIST: There is no reason for you to prefer them.

GAMBLER: Actually, these are the numbers of my personal address, and they have helped me win several times.

THERAPIST: Is there another reason?

GAMBLER: No.

The gambling session is sequentially dissected. All the gambler's actions and behavior are passed over with a fine tooth comb. Nothing is left unaccounted for.

THERAPIST: Once you had chosen your croupier, how did you begin to bet?
GAMBLER: Obviously, I made a large bet on the first turn.
THERAPIST: Why?
GAMBLER: Usually, when my observations are correct, I win every time.
THERAPIST: What do you mean by "correct observations"?
GAMBLER: It's a bit complicated to explain, but I calculate the time that has passed between bets. If I bet at the right time, then I win.
THERAPIST: Tell me more about the "right time", what does that mean?
GAMBLER: I think that it's good to vary bets according to a rhythm of one hour at a time. So, I increase the bets after each hour.
THERAPIST: Why after each hour?
GAMBLER: By doing so in the past, I won more often.

At several places in this dialogue, it would have been interesting to challenge the gambler's assertions. In fact, it is unlikely that the gambler won more often by using his "hourly rhythm" method. However, observation of the gambling session is not the time to challenge the gambler's ideas; it is more important to accompany the gambler's reasoning in order to track down, without his or her knowledge, as many errors in thinking as possible.

THERAPIST: Do you have other things that you do that will help me to better understand your way of gambling?
GAMBLER: No, I don't think so.
THERAPIST: We often hear that gamblers are superstitious, do you think you have any superstitions?
GAMBLER: No, none. I don't believe in those crazy ideas.
THERAPIST: Without being superstitious, some gamblers pray or have rituals...
GAMBLER: Not at all. I'm repulsed by the simplicity of such beliefs. I'm a very logical person.
THERAPIST: Tell me, in detail, all about this gambling session. What happened after your first bet?

At this stage, it is important to not presume anything. It is in this way that the therapist reconstructs, step by step, the entire recent gambling session. Once the description of the gambling session has ended, gamblers are invited to express what they were thinking while returning home.

THERAPIST: When you left the casino, what were you thinking?
GAMBLER: Because I lost $420, I told myself that I shouldn't have gone. I was mad at myself for having lost control.

Essentially, this is how the observation of a recent gambling session works. In the preceding excerpt, the descending arrow technique was applied to each of the gambler's assertions in order to reveal a maximum number of erroneous thoughts. With this technique, which is simple enough overall, it becomes relatively easy to discover most of the gambler's erroneous ideas. It consists of sounding out his or her assertions by way of sub-questions or secondary questions.

The cognitive approach and gambling

Following the identification of erroneous thoughts, the gambler is prepared to undergo cognitive therapy. Most of the time, gamblers possess a personal conception of the causes of their gambling excesses as well as how they would like to be thought of. Accordingly, it is suitable for therapists to adopt an attitude of healthy curiosity regarding this if they wish future interventions to be effective and to maintain the gambler's interest. Thus, the cognitive approach is presented to gamblers only once their ideas concerning the kind of treatment they would like to receive are heard.

THERAPIST: According to you, why did you develop this destructive passion for gambling?

GAMBLER: You know, I think that my gambling problem is due to my problematic relationship with my father. Since I was young, I've developed dependent relationships with people. Each time, it was like I was trying to get closer to my father, and I think that I repeat this pattern with video lotteries.

THERAPIST: Considering this, what are you expecting from a treatment for gambling?

GAMBLER: I would like to talk about the troublesome years of my childhood and free myself from this desire to get closer to my father. According to me, the cause of my gambling lies there.

THERAPIST: I'm convinced that it would be very important for you to understand the troublesome years of your childhood. It's just that I ask myself whether it is strategic to begin there? I think that the first thing for all gamblers to do is distance themselves from gaming locations. The second, and most important, is to take control over their desire to gamble. This is what cognitive therapy can offer. Then afterwards, you could undertake the process of exploring your childhood. What do you think?

For gamblers who do not expect to participate in a cognitive treatment, the idea of proceeding by steps reassures them without dismissing their personal conception of a treatment for gambling. Since they have often endured numerous failures and have little self-esteem, gamblers have difficulty believing in their ability to solve their gambling problem. The cognitive approach involves a change of perspective because it attempts to make the gamblers aware of and to stimulate feelings of mastery. With this in mind, the therapist presents to the gambler, the evocative image of the relationship between a lion-tamer and a lion, providing a clear and simple vision of the cognitive approach to excessive gambling.

THERAPIST: I would like you to consider the image of a lion, which is known to be a strong and powerful animal guided by instinct. When a lion-tamer attempts to make it obey, the lion naturally resists with all its strength…

It is only with perseverance that the lion-tamer is able to tame it. We all possess a lion and a lion-tamer within ourselves. Our logical or rational side may be considered our lion-tamer, while our instinct corresponds to the lion. Right now, your instinct for gambling is very strong and your lion continually roars. It is up to your lion-tamer to take control. With therapy, you will gain new tools to help you do so.

This image gives gamblers hope, since it allows them to see that they do have the ability to tame their excessive gambling behavior. It suggests that they are not without resources and that they can act upon their problem. The gambler's task, as a lion-tamer or the engine of change, consists of detecting and fighting off spontaneous erroneous thoughts in order to take control over his or her behavior.

It is important to convey a positive image of the gambler during this process, starting with the first meeting. When gamblers make the decision to consult a professional, they often feel overwhelmed. While they are conscious that they lose money, they realize that they always bet more. Faced with this obvious paradox and their total loss of control, they feel quite helpless. In fact, the absurdity of this behavior overwhelms and discourages them. Accordingly, over the course of therapy, gamblers are never viewed as sick persons. With the goal of increasing self-esteem, gambling excesses are not personalized, but rather presented as a loss of control associated with a destructive passion.

In order to help gamblers to control their problem, it is advisable to avoid the words "dependent", "compulsive", or "excessive". The gamblers must not feel like sick people who must be treated, but see themselves as agents that can apply new solutions in order to take control of a pervasive passion. Here, it is not a question of denying the seriousness of the problem, but to create a sane climate and a positive relationship between the gamblers and the resource people who accompany them in this new process of change. This is why, from the first few contacts on, the emphasis is put onto the erroneous character of thoughts and the possibility of modifying them, rather than on an excessive personality trait.

GAMBLER: How can it be that I'm so stupid? I see that I'm losing and I know that it's impossible for me to win back my money, and yet I persist.

THERAPIST: You know, there are several types of passion. For example, let's talk about passionate love. Who among us has not experienced the absurdity of a madly passionate relationship, even though we knew it was destined to fail? Would you say to me that passionate love is stupid? We are all passionate to various degrees and I would say that you are unlucky to have developed a destructive passion for gambling. You know, I often think that one does not choose who one loves.

Besides talking about destructive passion, one way of reinforcing gamblers' self-esteem is to emphasize their astonishing ability to adapt to their gambling problem. For example, gamblers are often transformed into well-informed consumers or learn, like soldiers lost in a forest, how to survive in the absence of means. Certain gamblers choose to live under the financial supervision of their spouse or to exclude themselves from casinos.

Describing the adaptation strategies that excessive gamblers develop as valorous is useful in building up and improving their self-image. This means that speaking of a destructive passion or the ability to adapt will only encourage the gamblers to pursue their goal of abstinence. Given the taboos around gambling as an addiction and the poor self-esteem of gamblers, requesting the assistance of a professional is the product of boldness. Thus, one shouldn't refrain from pointing out the courage of gamblers who ask for help.

At the beginning of therapy, gamblers often hope to be totally free of the desire to gamble. The loss of control is crippling. Gamblers are tormented and obsessed by gambling. Instead of promising such deliverance, the therapist warns them of probable variations in their desire to gamble. Given the difficulty involved with ceasing all gambling activities, it is preferable to refrain from making false promises. The therapist thus presents the gamblers with a realistic portrait of gambling cessation, as well as the emotive, familial, social, and financial difficulties that accompany change.

GAMBLER: Can you guarantee that I will no longer want to gamble when I leave therapy?

THERAPIST: I'm afraid that we won't be killing the lion and you should remain on the look-out. Rarely are there lion-tamers that are not distrustful of their lions. Throughout their lives, they remain vigilant, and that's what should be done since this fear ensures their survival. Without a lion, the lion-tamer no longer has a reason to be. Your instinct ensures your survival. On the other hand, what is important is that your lion-tamer take control over your lion.

GAMBLER: Does that mean that I will always be bothered by gambling?

THERAPIST: With time, your lion's roars will be less intense. On what, according to you, is the lion-tamer's pride based? Never hearing his lion's roars or being able to quiet them?

This type of dialogue orients gamblers towards the idea of controlling the desire to gamble using personal means, rather than maintaining the illusion of it disappearing like magic. This form of self-control represents the ultimate goal of cognitive therapy. Once this objective is clearly specified, the therapist will verify whether such a therapeutic process interests the gamblers.

Given the gamblers' ambivalence towards giving up gambling, it is appropriate to ascertain and stimulate the gamblers' adherence to treatment at the beginning of therapy. It is possible to opt for a paradoxical path, by indicating to the gamblers that there is a strong chance that they will not complete the treatment since one out of two individuals quit. The therapist can also say that there is a 50% chance of being among those who leave therapy before the end. This way of proceeding aims to stimulate the combative nature of gamblers and to provide them with the challenge of proving that they will not become one of those people who quit therapy. However, the opposite perspective is also viable. In this case, therapists and resource people prefer to speak of the success rate, which is approximately 85% of those who complete the therapy, in order to favor greater adherence to treatment.

The treatment

From the beginning of cognitive therapy, we ask the gambler to fill out a self-observation form concerning his or her gambling habits. With this personal data form, it is possible to observe slight variations in his or her gambling habits. This self-observation form is more than a simple photograph of a given moment. It is more like an x-ray since it allows, most notably, identification of the location and size of the discomfort. Self-observation also allows gamblers to monitor their progress. This data increases the gambler's motivation and helps to crystallize his or her desire to cease gambling.

This self-observation form constitutes the departure point for each meeting. Whether it consists of a minimal decrease in betting or the time spent gambling, each new positive element from this x-ray reinforces the gambler's motivation. Accordingly, the therapist highlights the gambler's inner dialogue and reinforces dialogue or ideas that are the basis for refusing to gamble.

THERAPIST: I see in your x-ray that you didn't go gambling on Friday despite a strong desire. What did you do in order to resist?

GAMBLER: I told myself that my children don't deserve for me to gamble like that. How I would like to give them the gift of not gambling any more!

THERAPIST: I encourage you to repeat those words as often as possible and with the same conviction. What you are saying inside of you influences your decisions.

This type of intervention emphasizes the relationship between the gambler's thoughts and the decision to not gamble. It highlights the cause–effect relation that unites thoughts and behavior. This way, the gambler is encouraged to consider the decisions he or she makes as well as the dialogue that accompanies these decisions. Within this example, the gambler realized that she abstained from gambling for a particular reason and that she can make this decision again in the future. Gambling then loses its insurmountable character and the gambler experiences a feeling of control.

As previously indicated, mastery of erroneous thoughts is the ultimate goal of therapy. But, how does the therapist steer the gambler to participate in the correction of erroneous thoughts without upsetting him or her? How do we invite the gambler's collaboration? In just a few steps, the treatment facilitates the transition from a system of erroneous thoughts to a system of thinking that is appropriate to the realities of gambling games.

"The Passion for Gambling"

At the beginning of therapy, an exercise is conducted to help the gambler look at his or her problem from a certain distance. "The Passion for Gambling" exercise consists of representing the space that gambling takes up within the gambler's life, by coloring in the interior of an empty circle. The colored-in portion indicates the extent to which gambling invades the gambler's universe. Most of the time, the gambler colors in between half and three-quarters of the circle.

When completing this exercise, the gambler frequently emphasizes the destructive nature of gambling. This most notably allows the gambler to express his or her obsession and to speak of the aspects of living that have been given up since gambling became the center of his or her universe. This exercise gives gamblers the opportunity to notice that they no longer invest in spousal, family, or social relationships. "The Passion for Gambling" exercise is often an ideal moment for the gamblers to realize that all their other passions or areas of interest have been consumed by gambling. Since the main objective of the exercise is the expression of emotions and feelings brought about by gambling, it is important to adopt an open attitude regarding what the gambler has to say.

The gambler's motivation exercise

After "The Passion for Gambling" exercise, the gambler helps to identify the obstacles that are likely to magnify or maintain his or her ambivalence towards the possibility of ending gambling activities. Several difficulties arise. First, gamblers rationally know that it is better to stop gambling, but the more they resist, the more their desire torments them. This dilemma creates ambivalence about ceasing gambling and increases the risks of relapse. How can the therapist help the gambler to be freed from this inner pressure? The following exercise concerning the gambler's motivation pertains to the consequences of giving up or continuing to participate in gambling activities. In this exercise, the gambler inventories the pros and cons to the cessation and pursuit of gambling activities. Gamblers that realize the consequences and their scope, improve their ability to focus on their goal of quitting gambling. Since the gambler's ambivalence is often at the bottom of his or her relapses, dedicating an important part of the session to the completion of this exercise on motivation is worthwhile.

- Pros of gambling (positive consequences of gambling)
- Cons of giving up gambling (what I will lose if I stop gambling)
- Cons of gambling (the negative consequences of gambling)
- Pros of giving up gambling (what I will gain if I stop gambling)

Pros of gambling
(positive consequences of gambling)

The first part of this exercise consists of listing everything that the gambler considers advantageous about gambling. In response to this question, gamblers will spontaneously reply that there is nothing good to be gained from gambling and they will support their reasoning with the fact that they are in therapy. However, if we invite gamblers to ask themselves, for example, about the occasions that gambling offers for escape, they may realize that gambling is a moment of solitude, a way of letting go of frustrations, an escape from problems, a way of rapidly paying back debts, or a way of treating oneself. The pleasure and euphoria that wins provoke, as well as the possibility of recuperating losses, are also mentioned often by numerous gamblers. However, when identifying the advantages of gambling, the therapist should acknowledge them, as it is also important to highlight their futility.

Sooner or later, gamblers will turn their backs to the positive consequences of gambling. In order to avoid exacerbating the already present feeling of emptiness that is sure to accompany the cessation of gambling, the gambler is invited to seek out activities that can replace gambling. In fact, it is idealistic to attempt to suppress a harmful behavior without ensuring that it is replaced by another behavior that will improve the gambler's quality of life. Accordingly, the gambler's previous interests that were abandoned in lieu of gambling (such as golf, bowling, or reading) are suggested. It is important to note here that, throughout therapy, interventions allowing for the positive modification of the gambler's behavior are most welcome.

Cons of giving up gambling
(what I will lose if I stop gambling)

Giving up gambling has certain negative consequences and it is in the gambler's best interest to know what they are. Quitting gambling marks the beginning of a new perspective on life, and the gambler must entirely reconstruct his or her life. This great challenge is associated with numerous worries and a great deal of stress.

GAMBLER: I'll find it hard to stop. In fact, it's obvious that if I stop, I'll have more and more money in the bank. This money will bother me because I'll tell myself that I could bet it.

This last quotation well illustrates the obsessive nature of gambling and alludes to the numerous traps that await the gambler who attempts to abstain from gambling. In fact, ceasing gambling means that the gambler must reject the very idea of recuperating losses and recognize past monetary losses. The decision to stop gambling often forces gamblers to confront other difficulties in their life, and over a long period of time, to reorganize their existence. For example, gamblers who are newly abstinent often find themselves faced with unpleasant realities. It is possible that because of gambling, gamblers lost their spouse, distanced themselves from their family, abandoned their friends, sold their house, and quit their job. In brief, the gambler's entire life needs to be reconstructed.

The gambler who decides to quit gambling is renouncing a behavior that is familiar. He or she recognizes that gambling can no longer be considered as a solution for emotional or financial difficulties, even on a short-term basis. Is gambling a problem for the gambler, or a solution? This question often has a therapeutic effect on gamblers. If they are consulting a therapist, it is probably because they consider their gambling behavior to be a stumbling block and not merely an interesting pastime. However, awakening gamblers to the fact that they sometimes perceive gambling as a viable option in the short term, brings them face to face with a contradiction: they are consulting a specialist because they want to be freed of the chains of gambling, but they use gambling as a way of over-coming certain difficulties.

Normally, solutions solve problems, but, in the case of excessive gambling, resorting to gambling as a short-term solution only exacerbates the situation. For example, is it effective to lose oneself in the activity of gambling in order to overcome distress resulting from loneliness? Is that what the gambler wants? Over the course of this discussion, the gambler realizes that giving up gambling can only be effective if he or she admits to being beaten and considers gambling as the real problem and not as a short-term solution. One gambler's remarks at the beginning of therapy speak well of her apprehension about the difficulties associated with ceasing gambling activities.

GAMBLER: You know, it's difficult to stop gambling. It's like my relationship with my husband that has not been going well for a long time. I've invested so much in it that I can't abandon it now. I keep hoping that my spouse will soon change and things will go back to the way they were at the beginning of our relationship. Every time I get even a little attention from him, I tell myself "there you go, your efforts are paying off". I truly think that with perseverance, we can accomplish anything. If I end this relationship, I would have to admit that all my efforts were a waste of time and that I made a serious mistake. In fact, I would feel stupid.

Cons of gambling
(the negative consequences of gambling)

The gamblers' ambivalence towards giving up gambling is what lets them minimize or ignore the reality of their problems. To highlight the contrast between the advantages and disadvantages of gambling, gamblers are invited to list the negative consequences associated with excessive gambling. This exercise allows gamblers to explore the real damages caused by gambling. Gamblers spontaneously identify a great number of cons, among which we find loss of self-esteem, shame, laziness, isolation, lies, hypocrisy, loss of trust from friends and family, interpersonal conflicts, couple difficulties, extreme stress as a result of monetary losses, time lost while trying to recuperate money, shifting of values, risk of break-up, risk of losing their job, obsessions, and insomnia. Gamblers might also mention that they bet money destined for their fundamental needs, that they eat poorly and that they deprive their children of certain needs. Furthermore, gamblers can still name several other negative consequences of gambling when ending this exercise.

GAMBLER: Since I've been in my gambling world, I've neglected myself. I don't have enough money to buy new clothes, or to see the dentist or hairstylist. I no longer go to the movies or restaurants. In fact, I'm at the point of depriving myself of everything except gambling. I save to go gambling and I see necessary purchases as a waste. I even deprive myself of lunchtime coffee since that $1 could be the one that will win me the jackpot. I have lost control over my life and this loss of control has spread. I've even reached the point of stealing from my own children.

It is important to encourage discussion about the negative consequences of excessive gambling for two reasons. The first is that gamblers often do not have occasions to speak about their problems because their passion for gambling is clouded by shame and secrecy. Thus, it is a prime opportunity for them to express what they feel. The second reason is based on the hypothesis that the more gamblers recognize the negative consequences of gambling on their lives, as well as the lives of their friends and family, the better are their chances that they will persevere in their pursuit to cease gambling. In this sense, this exercise can be considered a time of disclosure and unveiling.

Regarding the negative consequences of gambling, the gambler is invited to question the potential consequences of continuing to gamble. In order to do this, gamblers are asked to project themselves into the future and to describe what their lives would be like if they were to continue to gamble. The somber perspective that results might, in certain cases, be useful and exploited during moments of strong ambivalence.

Pros of giving up gambling
(what I will gain if I stop gambling)

The advantages of giving up gambling are brought to the fore over the course of this discussion. At this point in the exercise, gamblers may mention that they desire a return of their self-esteem and underlying values. They wish to be freed of the anxiety, depression, anger, and obsessions brought on by gambling. They also indicate that stopping gambling would allow them to recover control over their lives and to maintain a budget. For them, the adoption of this new lifestyle would allow them to exchange their feelings of shame for feelings of pride. Additionally, gamblers can attempt to renew their relationships with the people they love and to re-involve themselves, without hypocrisy, in interpersonal relationships based on confidence and unselfishness.

By quitting gambling, gamblers aspire to rediscover a lifestyle that suits them. This desire, which is one of the many advantages associated with giving up gambling, is examined at length with gamblers. Accordingly, they are invited to imagine themselves in the future and to foresee what their life would be like if they no longer gambled. It is advisable to suggest projections that support a simple modification of behavior. For example, the therapist can ask the gambler to describe a small behavior change that would result from the cessation of gambling. The therapist counts on the fact that the more gamblers acquire new life habits, the less they will be obsessed by the desire to gamble and, consequently, the more these new habits will become reflexive.

GAMBLER: Since I've been gambling, I forgot about the pleasures of going for coffee and doing crosswords in a restaurant. When I overcome my gambling problems, I'll do those things again.

THERAPIST: Could you, from this week on, adopt those habits again? Do you believe that you have to wait until your gambling problem is resolved before you can do those things again?

Gamblers are sometimes prone to depreciate the exercise by saying they are already aware of the pros of continuing or ceasing gambling, since all one needs to do is take the opposite of the cons. Gamblers must be reminded that it is just as important to pursue short- and medium-term objectives; it is necessary to turn the negative consequences of gambling into positive aims.

Over the course of this same exercise, it is also important for gamblers to write down their personal reasons for ceasing to gamble. If they choose to stop gambling, it should be for precise and well thought-out motives – for reasons that they know and recognize. If they remain focused on these reasons, they will find more strength to resist the urge to gamble. The exercise is much more effective when gamblers convince themselves using their own motives, understanding exactly why they choose to give up gambling and what they have to gain by ceasing to gamble. Thinking about both the negative consequences of choosing to gamble and the advantages of giving up gambling will certainly have more impact than simply prohibiting oneself from gambling or telling oneself not to gamble. The former route supposes a thought-out decision, while the latter is based on a sense of obligation or a denial of pleasure.

In short, the motivation exercise lets gamblers make a complete inventory of what is involved in the pursuit and the cessation of gambling. Through it, they can understand why they want to stop gambling and determine the goals they wish to pursue. Furthermore, this exercise sheds light on elements that might create feelings of ambivalence over the course of therapy.

Chance

The next step in treatment consists of making gamblers aware of the concept of chance. It is rather surprising to note that the large majority of people who succumb to these games do not know the meaning of the word "chance". In this step of the therapy, the gamblers and therapist work together in order to establish an accurate definition of "chance". This is because gamblers' errors in thinking are most often based on inaccurate knowledge or a misunderstanding of the concept.

THERAPIST: Your passion for gambling is directed towards games of chance and money. I'm convinced that you know what money is. However, can you tell me what the word "chance" means?

GAMBLER: I don't understand what you want to know...

THERAPIST: I'd like you to explain what the word "chance" means, as if you had to define it to a 6-year-old child.

GAMBLER: Chance, it's like when we don't know beforehand what will happen. It's luck.

THERAPIST: Do you think that all chances are happy events? If, by chance, a man is attacked on the road, would you say that it was a lucky event?

GAMBLER: That's true. Chance is when one cannot know in advance what is coming or what will happen. It can be lucky or unlucky!

Over the course of their discussion about chance, the therapist has in mind its definition: i.e., all unforeseen or unpredictable events over which a person has no control. Furthermore, when the gambler proposes a definition that appears to be accurate, the therapist invites him or her to write it down. In the previous excerpt, the gambler made the classic mistake of confusing the word "chance" with the word "luck" at the beginning. But, the gambler quickly managed to formulate a correct definition of chance. As rapid as the process is, it is a decisive step in the treatment since the gambler will be invited to revisit this definition throughout therapy.

Next, the therapist verifies whether the gambler confuses games of skill and games of chance. In a game of skill, gamblers can improve their technique and influence results in their favor. For example, the more they play pool, the better they become and the more they increase their chances of winning against opponents. Conversely, with games of chance, it is impossible for somebody to improve enough to change the result. If it were otherwise, we would have to acknowledge that we could somehow act to affect chance. This does not respect the definition of chance as an unforeseeable event. Accordingly, gamblers cannot improve on chance or master it. We are all equally powerless before chance and absolutely nothing can alter this implacable law.

Once gamblers understand the difference between chance and skill, the therapist prepares them to work on their thoughts. Because the objective of therapy is to allow gamblers to recognize and modify the erroneous thoughts that incite them to gamble, gamblers are encouraged to identify the situations that can result in relapse.

Risky situations

Several situations awaken the desire to gamble and increase the risks of returning to it. Over the course of treatment, gamblers learn to detect these risky situations and they are asked to list them. By doing so, the gamblers train themselves to recognize these as situations of which to be wary.

If gamblers have difficulties recognizing situations that trigger their desire to gamble, the therapist can suggest a few. Some situations that can trigger the urge to gamble include: lottery advertisements, emotions generated by conflict, alcohol consumption, winning or losing money, payday, outstanding bills, and rumors about video lottery terminals from which nobody has won a jackpot for a long time.

Gamblers have little or no control over risky situations, therefore, they can never completely avoid them. There is an abundance of casinos and gambling establishments. Sooner or later, gamblers must face them. It is thus to their advantage that they learn to control themselves. But, how can therapists help gamblers to control a desire to gamble that is triggered by risky situations that arise in everyday life? By invoking the notion of choice. When gamblers realize that risky situations generate the thoughts that underlie their decision to go gambling, they can then train themselves to recognize those thoughts whenever they find themselves in a risky situation.

THERAPIST: A fondue pot can explode and cause much injury. We could consider that to be a risky situation. But, you may have noticed that not all fondue pots explode, right? In order for it to explode, you need to throw oil at it.

Applying this illustration, gamblers come to associate their erroneous thoughts with oil that is thrown at a fondue pot. In order to assess their comprehension of this process, the therapist invites the gamblers to relate a risky situation and a thought that gives them the urge to gamble. By doing so, gamblers identify the thoughts that arise when they face a risky situation.

GAMBLER: For me, a risky situation is when I'm bored and I have a little bit of money on me. Inevitably, I tell myself that I could go to the casino and bet $20. If I understand correctly, my thought is when I tell myself that?

Gamblers are made aware of the role that thoughts play in the decision-making process. Clearly defining the relationship between what gamblers think and the choices they make that guide their behavior is the central element of therapy. Within this perspective, thoughts can be compared to danger signs.

THERAPIST: A video lottery advertisement isn't dangerous in itself. If that were the case, we would all have serious gambling problems. However, it can create an urge to gamble among certain people. Even then, desire alone does not decide for us. For example, I could want to leave for Las Vegas but decide to never get there. What produces our behavior is the final decision we make, and this decision takes place in our thoughts.

The excessive gambling chain of thoughts

The vicious circle of excessive gambling is presented to the gambler in the form of an explanatory model. This model provides a visual reference that represents for the dynamics of the excessive gambler. Upon being shown this model, gamblers are often able to recognize themselves within it. In this regard, the excessive gambling chain of thought is reassuring for gamblers as it suggests an evolution or a process that is identical for the majority of gamblers.

Use of this model, which is reproduced in Chapter 3, allows the gambler to understand that passing from one stage to the next is accompanied by erroneous thoughts most of the time. For example, gamblers who cannot control themselves after a first bet of $20, firmly believe that they will win a jackpot if they continue to gamble. Continuing to bet after an important win indicates the presence of another erroneous idea. This model helps gamblers to identify their own ideas about gambling in general, as well as within particular gambling sessions. Gamblers understand, via the chain model, that erroneous ideas become stronger farther down the chain. The more the gambler ventures into the links of this chain, the more it is difficult for him or her to stop gambling without leaving all his or her money behind. This is why it is important for gamblers to be well informed of the fact that risky situations, which trigger the desire to gamble, provide the best opportunity to identify and modify their erroneous thoughts. Gamblers who find themselves in a risky situation and who recognize the thoughts that drive them to gamble at the time, considerably increase their chances of making the decision to abstain from gambling.

The "Let's play" exercises

Once gamblers understand what errors in thinking are and the consequences these have on decisions, they are then able to undertake exercises that challenge erroneous thoughts. Challenging erroneous thoughts is the essence of the entire therapeutic process. In order to support their decision to no longer gamble, gamblers work at modifying spontaneous thoughts that incite them to gamble or that encourage them to continue gambling. These practical exercises allow gamblers to organize their thoughts and to act upon them. As well, the more they complete these exercises, the more they become capable of resisting their desire to gamble. In fact, through these exercises, gamblers learn to no longer let themselves be trapped by risky situations and by the erroneous ideas they provoke.

An excellent way to help gamblers to overcome their urge to gamble consists of bringing them to recognize the relationship between their thoughts and decisions. As mentioned previously, at the beginning of each therapy session gamblers relate the occasions where they managed to abstain from gambling despite a strong impulse to gamble. They question themselves about the ideas that allowed them to overcome their desire. Once they have isolated these thoughts, gamblers regularly remember them. The gamblers then attribute a form of mastery over them and are freed from the feelings of powerlessness that paralyzed them for so long. They realize, little by little, that they have the power to rebel against their desire to gamble.

The "Let's play" exercises promote recognition and integration of the relationship between thoughts and the decision whether to gamble or not. This exercise reduces ambivalence towards gambling and allows the gambler to perceive abstinence as an informed choice rather than as a deprivation. The objective of the exercise is to discover and modify gamblers' spontaneous thoughts, which form the basis of their decision to gamble. With time and much training, gamblers becomes skilled at replacing their old mental reflexes by new thoughts geared towards their personal objective to quit gambling.

In order to complete the "Let's play" exercises, gamblers do not have to have had a relapse. Simply finding themselves within a risky situation allows them to develop their skills for detecting and modifying their erroneous thoughts. Generally, at the time of their therapy sessions, gamblers complete the "Let's play" exercise based on the last risky situation they encountered or their latest relapse. The therapist's role consists of guiding gamblers' reflections in a way that recognizes risky situations and the erroneous ideas they trigger. The gamblers' task is to identify the thoughts that will help them to attain and maintain abstinence. Different types of intervention are possible in order to achieve this treatment goal.

In this exercise, gamblers take each of their erroneous thoughts and replace them with thoughts that more accurately reflect the realities of gambling and that are in line with their objective of ceasing to gamble. They write down the new ideas in the column representing thoughts that give them control over their desire to gamble. Similar to training for a sport, practice and perseverance often represent a good prognosis of success. The more the gambler entertains new appropriate thoughts, the less he or she succumbs to a desire to gamble. This is why gamblers will complete as many "Let's play" exercises as there are times when they have felt the urge to gamble or have faced a risky situation.

Each meeting begins with an examination of the exercises that the gamblers have completed. If they have not done any, the therapist takes advantage of the time to reassess the degree of ambivalence towards treatment. The therapist then asks the gamblers to do a new exercise based on a risky situation that occurred during the past week. Completing these types of exercises allows the gamblers and their resource persons to remain focused on treatment goals. The following is a short excerpt of an interview that focus on how to complete this exercise. The gambler begins by describing the risky situation. Next, he or she identifies the spontaneous thoughts that it triggered.

THERAPIST: Do you remember me telling you that your lion-tamer can take control over the lion? The exercise I'm proposing aims to increase your control over your urge to gamble. What was the situation that gave you the desire to go gambling on Friday?

GAMBLER: On my way home from work, I saw my favorite bar in the distance.

THERAPIST: Do you remember saying something to yourself at that time?

GAMBLER: Not really, I saw the bar.

THERAPIST: Would you say that seeing the bar was a risky situation for you?

GAMBLER: Certainly. When I saw it, all my good resolutions flew out the window.

THERAPIST: Could you write this situation under the "Risky situation" column?

GAMBLER: So I write, "see my favorite bar". (See Table 5.1)

Table 5.1: The "Let's play" exercise

Risky situation	Spontaneous thoughts that give me the urge to gamble	Thoughts that give me control over my urge to gamble	What do I choose to do instead?
See my favorite bar.			

THERAPIST: We will now try to find the thoughts that came to you when you saw the bar and that gave you the urge to gamble. When you saw the bar, you said it gave you the desire. What exactly did you have the desire for?

GAMBLER: I had the desire to think of nothing. It was a hard week and I was very stressed. I needed to feel good."

THERAPIST: What motivated you to gamble was in fact the desire you had to feel good.

GAMBLER: That's it exactly. Friday evening, it's often the same scenario: I'm stressed and I need to gamble in order to calm myself down.

THERAPIST: Could you write what you just mentioned to me below it? This thought of decreasing your stress and the desire to feel good seem to be strongly associated to the fact that you gambled. (See Table 5.2)

Table 5.2: The "Let's play" exercise

Risky situation	Spontaneous thoughts that give me the urge to gamble	Thoughts that give me control over my urge to gamble	What do I choose to do instead?
See my favorite bar.	1. *"I told myself that I needed to feel good and that I needed to gamble in order to do so."*		

THERAPIST: What do you mean by "I needed to gamble in order do so"?

In order to assist gamblers with recognizing their erroneous thoughts, the therapist undertakes an interrogation using the descending arrow technique. After each of the gambler's comments, the therapist asks a sub-question to try to bring out ideas that encourage the urge to gamble. The therapist tries to get the gamblers to express thoughts concerning their conviction in winning or attempts to predict outcomes.

GAMBLER: Well, as soon as I begin gambling, I forget all my problems and my stress goes away. It's really the best way for me to think about nothing.

THERAPIST: Could you write that down? (See Table 5.3)

Table 5.3: The "Let's play" exercise

Risky situation	Spontaneous thoughts that give me the urge to gamble	Thoughts that give me control over my urge to gamble	What do I choose to do instead?
See my favorite bar.	1. "I told myself that I needed to feel [...]" 2. *"I tell myself that all my stress will go away and that there is nothing better for me to do when I want to forget everything."*		

THERAPIST: How could you know that your stress would decrease? Gambling sessions don't always have happy outcomes you know.

GAMBLER: Yes, I know. However, it was as though I felt like I would win. In fact, I felt an "electric" sensation go through my body.

THERAPIST: This electric sensation leads you to believe you are going to win?

GAMBLER: Yes.

THERAPIST: Could you write that down? (See Table 5.4)

Table 5.4: The "Let's play" exercise

Risky situation	Spontaneous thoughts that give me the urge to gamble	Thoughts that give me control over my urge to gamble	What do I choose to do instead?
See my favorite bar.	1. "I told myself that I needed to feel [...]" 2. "I tell myself that all my stress will go away [...]" 3. *"I tell myself that the electric sensation going through my body indicates that I will win."*		

The gambler's conviction of winning is quickly revealed. The next task is to discover the erroneous ideas that manifest themselves during that same gambling session. The therapist asks about behaviors in which the gambler engaged and the thoughts that accompanied them. The gambler can then become aware of his or her illusions of control and errors of perception regarding independence of turns.

THERAPIST: Following this electric sensation, how did you choose your video lottery terminal?

GAMBLER: Since a lady just lost a large sum of money at that video terminal, I told myself that I couldn't be unlucky all evening. Moreover, I needed to win and I deserved to. My week was impossible and not everything could go wrong in it.

THERAPIST: All these spontaneous thoughts seem to amplify your desire to gamble. Could you write them on your sheet? (See Table 5.5)

Table 5.5: The "Let's play" exercise

Risky situation	Spontaneous thoughts that give me the urge to gamble	Thoughts that give me control over my urge to gamble	What do I choose to do instead?
See my favorite bar.	1. "I told myself that I needed to feel […]"		
	2. "I tell myself that all my stress will go away […]"		
	3. "I tell myself that the electric […]"		
	4. *"I told myself that not everything could go wrong. Furthermore, the machine is full and I deserve to win."*		

THERAPIST: Thus, you began to gamble. How much money did you bet from the start and why?

GAMBLER: I always start with $10. I like to test the machine before adventuring towards larger bets. Since it was often paying out little wins, I knew at that time that it would be a good one. I thus increased my bets and stayed on that machine.

THERAPIST: Take the time to write that down please. (See Table 5.6)

In a therapy session, this exercise continues until gamblers have completely covered their last relapse. When the main erroneous thoughts that occurred before, during, and after the gambling session are revealed, it is suggested to the gamblers that they question them and, using a series of questions, we invite them to examine their initial ideas. It is at this step of the exercise that the therapist asks the gamblers' lion-tamer to intervene.

THERAPIST: You have just listed the spontaneous thoughts present before, during, and after your last gambling session. Your work now consists of finding a way of seeing things that distances you from gambling. Let's continue the exercise. The first thought that gave you the urge to gamble corresponds to the idea that you need to gamble in order to feel good. Could you write down a thought that would help you thwart this idea

Table 5.6: The "Let's play" exercise

Risky situation	Spontaneous thoughts that give me the urge to gamble	Thoughts that give me control over my urge to gamble	What do I choose to do instead?
See my favorite bar.	1. "I told myself that I needed to feel [...]"		
	2. "I tell myself that all my stress will go away [...]"		
	3. "I tell myself that the electric [...]"		
	4. "I told myself that not everything could go wrong. [...]"		
	5. *"I tell myself that when the machine pays out small wins, I know that it will be a good machine."*		

and that would bring you closer to your objective of giving up gambling? (See Table 5.7)

Table 5.7: The "Let's play" exercise

Risky situation	Spontaneous thoughts that give me the urge to gamble	Thoughts that give me control over my urge to gamble	What do I choose to do instead?
See my favorite bar.	1. "I told myself that I needed to feel good and that I needed to gamble in order to do so."	1. *"I forget that gambling makes me experience negative emotions most of the time!"*	

By guiding gamblers, the therapist helps them to discover thoughts that focus on their quest for self-control. The therapist ensures that gamblers find new thoughts that truly speak to them: thoughts that have a personal value for the gambler. It is not enough that gamblers rationalize in such a way as to please the therapist, but that they discover a new way of thinking that will give them back their feeling of self-control.

THERAPIST: The second spontaneous thought alludes to gambling as an ideal solution. Could you see this in a way that would bring you closer to your objective of abstaining from gambling? (See Table 5.8)

Table 5.8: The "Let's play" exercise

Risky situation	Spontaneous thoughts that give me the urge to gamble	Thoughts that give me control over my urge to gamble	What do I choose to do instead?
See my favorite bar.	1. "I told myself that I needed to feel [...]"	1. "I forget that gambling makes me experience [...]"	
	2. "I tell myself that all my stress will go away and that there is nothing better for me to do when I want to forget everything."	2. *"My stress will decrease only if I win. I am a lot more likely to lose than win, and there is a great risk that I will find myself even more stressed after gambling. I have to stop seeing gambling as a solution. Also, if I win, I will want to return to gambling and my goal is to abstain."*	

It often happens that gamblers are unable to comfortably counteract some thoughts. For example, it is not obvious that the gambler can compensate for the third erroneous idea: "I tell myself that the electric sensation going through my body indicates that I will win." It is likely that he still believes that this electric sensation is, for him, a way of making efficacious predictions. In this case, it is possible to lead the gambler to doubt this perception by reminding him or her of the definition of chance he or she formulated at the beginning of therapy. Remember that at this stage, gamblers have already agreed that chance involves the inability to predict events. Gamblers who recognize this relationship will very often abandon the idea of being able to make such predictions.

However, what can one do when the gambler's belief seems unshakable? Since the objective of this exercise is the modification of erroneous ideas, the therapist must attempt to put doubt in the gambler's mind and demonstrate the inexactness of his assertion. For example, is the electric sensation that the gambler feels an effective way of predicting? Has the gambler previously lost after this sensation had occurred? Has he ever won without having felt this electric sensation beforehand? In order to identify these occasions where the gambler's certainty was undermined, the therapist gives the gambler as much time as necessary to respond. This method of proceeding creates contradictions within the gambler's mind since, most of the time, wins and losses are independent of what is felt beforehand. In most cases, the gambler recognizes the absence of predictive value in the sensation examined and considers modifying his or her idea.

If the certainty associated to the sensation remains unshakable, the therapist asks the gambler to complete a systematic observation exercise, which aims to compare his or her wins and losses as a function of the feelings experienced before the gambling sessions, should a relapse ensue. This exercise is generally enough to make the gambler realize that his physiological and emotional sensations in no way assist him in predicting wins. If, contrary to expectations, the gambler persists in saying that the electric sensation he feels is of great predictive value, the therapist then challenges the gambler's "reality" and asks him how it is that with such a method of prediction, he experiences so many financial losses. Moreover, why does he not only go gambling when he feels these sensations? Usually, this type of question leads to serious doubt concerning the initial idea and gamblers learn to distrust traps of this kind.

The last part of this exercise permits gamblers to evaluate the erroneous or correct character of their assertions. The cognitive work it involves does not aim to confront; rather, it is presented as a means of recovering control over their behavior. Hopefully, gamblers will generalize this way of questioning themselves to other areas of their lives. (See Table 5.9)

Table 5.9: The "Let's play" exercise

Risky situation	Spontaneous thoughts that give me the urge to gamble	Thoughts that give me control over my urge to gamble	What do I choose to do instead?
See my favorite bar.	1. "I told myself that I needed to feel [...]"	1. "I forget that gambling makes me experience [...]"	
	2. "I tell myself that all my stress will go away [...]"	2. "My stress will decrease only if I win. [...]"	
	3. "I tell myself that the electric sensation going through my body indicates that I will win."	3. *All of this is nothing but a trap. Chance bars prediction. I have often lost even when I felt an electric sensation.*	

Gamblers pursue the exercise by writing down new ideas that help them to dominate their desire to gamble. They could write, for example, that there is no relationship between their emotions and the machines' returns. Thus, they realize that the notion of deservingness has no effect on their chances of winning or that it is even absurd to say that a "full" machine should soon pay out. Gamblers also notice that nothing can help them to predict a win, or that testing a machine is completely pointless since each draw in video lottery is completely independent.

Gamblers finally arrive at an extremely important step in this exercise. They must choose what they will do the next time the risky situation presents itself. In the example we are using, the gambler decides that, the next time the risky situation arises, he will invite a friend out to a restaurant. (See Table 5.10)

Table 5.10: The "Let's play" exercise

Risky situation	Spontaneous thoughts that give me the urge to gamble	Thoughts that give me control over my urge to gamble	What do I choose to do instead?
See my favorite bar.	1. "I told myself that I needed to feel [...]"	1. "I forget that gambling makes me experience [...]"	*"I CHOOSE to have coffee with my friend the next time I find myself in this risky situation."*

Though they will be applying cognitive strategies, gamblers retain their freedom to determine their behavior, just as they assume responsibility for the consequences. Gamblers' choices and their freedom to prefer certain behaviors to others are, in fact, points that should be emphasized. Gamblers are responsible for their behavior and the therapist takes great care to mention this. At this step, it could be beneficial for gamblers to distinguish between pleasure and freedom. Freedom does not involve the ability to continually experience pleasure. This attitude creates more slavery. We need only think about alcoholics or drug addicts to understand that pleasure in the short run is not a sign of liberty. Rather, it rests on the people's ability to make choices that are good for them and to stop making choices that do not respect their own values or allow them to attain their life goals. Freedom also involves being responsible for the consequences of one's choices. By considering the notion of choice and freedom from this particular angle, gamblers understand that the decision to not gamble arises from personal liberty and not an exterior constraint.

By means of this exercise, gamblers always become more sensitive to what motivates them and are able to link their erroneous thoughts to their urge to gamble. Our experience reveals that the more a gambler is committed to completing these types of exercises, the more his or her ambivalence decreases. While there exists a multitude of risky situations and erroneous ideas, we can see what an example of a "Let's play" exercise looks like once finished. (See Table 5.11)

Table 5.11: The "Let's play" exercise

Risky situation	Spontaneous thoughts that give me the urge to gamble	Thoughts that give me control over my urge to gamble	What do I choose to do instead
Receive a bill	1. "I tell myself that as long as I don't have any money, I might as well take the chance of making some."	1. "I let myself be fooled by the lure of winning. If I continue to wear a blindfold and to live only with the hope of making short-term gains, I am guaranteed to continue losing more money. It is impossible for me to recuperate my losses. I know that. Also, I have a lot more chances of losing than of winning. The small amount of money I have is essential. Do I want a lack of money to become my lifestyle? Furthermore, I can tell myself that I am taking a risk and not a chance."	"I make the choice to not go gambling. Instead I will take those $20 and use them to give myself true pleasure. I will go to the movies and buy myself a good coffee. I will be more proud of myself!"
	2. "I also tell myself that we are at the beginning of the month and that the machines are full. I should thus come out a winner."	2. "Whether the machines are full or empty changes nothing. Each turn is new and my chances will never increase."	
	3. "I also tell myself I have nothing to lose."	3. "I have lots to lose, and …"	

Role playing and listening to the session

Other types of exercises can be carried out to enrich the preceding exercise. For example, when gamblers are able to re-evaluate or to reconsider their own thoughts, it is interesting to reverse the therapist and gambler's roles.

The gambler is then in the position of the one who must recognize the erroneous ideas proposed by the real therapist. The activity takes place in exactly the same way as the "Let's play" exercises. The therapist relates a risky situation, while the gambler systematically questions him or her in order to discover erroneous thoughts. Using this role-playing game, gamblers experience a powerful mirror effect because they recognize evidence of their erroneous ideas with regards to games of chance. This exercise is simple, amusing, and generally well appreciated by gamblers.

Another simple and efficacious way of reassessing erroneous thoughts consists of recording gamblers' dialogue on an audio-tape when they are describing their last relapse. The gamblers then listen to the recording and are invited to detect and correct their erroneous thoughts on their own.

6

TREATMENT OF THE EXCESSIVE GAMBLER: THE BEHAVIORAL APPROACH

While cognitive interventions constitute, without a doubt, the main and essential ingredient of the therapy, it is also necessary to provide gamblers with tools to deal with difficulties they encounter. This can be done by putting into place concrete measures that will help them to confront and deal with their problems effectively.

The difficulties gamblers often face take on the form of situations that increase the risk of relapse. If, with the assistance of cognitive interventions, gamblers develop a more realistic perception of gambling, they can better resist their desire to gamble. However, social, professional, and monetary difficulties might, unfortunately, compromise the desired balance and keep gamblers vulnerable to gambling.

We will now present certain risky situations as well as behavioral interventions that allow the gambler to deal with them. We have divided these risky situations into five categories: exposure to gambling, financial situation, relationship problems, free time, and consuming alcohol or drugs. The final section will address the issue of problems in daily life, and a list of strategies are proposed that are likely to help the gambler to attain the ultimate goal: abstinence from gambling. It goes without saying that without cognitive interventions, these strategies offer only a limited degree of effectiveness, and it is for this reason that we use them complementarily to cognitive treatment.

Risky situations and associated strategies

It is first important to re-emphasize the idea that risky situations do not lead to gambling, but rather the erroneous thoughts that risky situations provoke. The good news is that gamblers can directly act upon these situations as well as work on modifying their thoughts.

Exposure to gambling

Being in a gambling establishment obviously represents an important risky situation. If gamblers persistently frequent these places, they repeatedly foster their urge to gamble and make it difficult to resist. Given the increasing availability and accessibility of gambling games, it is unrealistic to think that one can continually avoid them. However, we know that gamblers can voluntarily bar themselves from some gaming establishments. This is certainly the first action to take when gamblers wish to cease gambling.

Certain casinos offer a program that allows gamblers to ban themselves from the establishment. In these self-exclusion programs, the gamblers meet the establishment's security service and sign a self-exclusion form. Their photo is also taken so that security can identify them if they try to enter the establishment again. The duration of self-exclusions varies according to the gambler's request and the norms in place within the casino. Certain contracts last a few months, while others extend over several years. This measure can be extremely effective as, out of fear of being identified and being subjected to the humiliation of expulsion, many gamblers give up going to the casino altogether.

However, what can be done if certain establishments do not offer this type of program? We can suggest to gamblers that they meet the managers of the establishment where they have the habit of gambling to explain their problem and ask that their access to the location be prohibited. There is no guarantee: if certain owners are willing to assist the gamblers in their process, others can very well refuse to comply with this request.

Self-exclusion is, without a doubt, the first strategy to employ in order to avoid exposure to gambling. Gamblers who reject this step experience ambivalence. They can refuse this option, asserting that control must first and foremost come from themselves or, if they self-exclude, the only thought that will come to mind upon expiration of his contract would be to hasten towards a gaming establishment. Even if self-exclusion appears to be a drastic solution, it can prove to be a strong tool for gamblers. It becomes a valuable ally, a weapon that protects gamblers until they are in a better position to modify their thoughts.

However, if it is impossible for gamblers to self-exclude from certain establishments, they should expect to confront numerous situations that risk exposing them to gambling. Here are some strategies that will help gamblers to deal with these situations.

Finding oneself near a gambling establishment
Gamblers frequently report that they gamble after work most of the time. Because they generally take the same route home, they have difficulty

preventing themselves from stopping at their usual place of gambling. In this case, it would be useful to suggest to gamblers that they:

- change their routes and ensure that the gambling establishment is not on their way home from work;
- systematically avoid going to places where it is possible for them to gamble. If, despite everything, they insist on going to bars, it would be preferable that they only go to those where there are no video lottery terminals.

Other gamblers plan their vacations according to the proximity of casinos or take cruises that have casinos on board. To these gamblers, we suggest that they reconsider their vacation projects and change their destinations.

Finding oneself in a gambling establishment
If gamblers find themselves in a gambling establishment despite their attempts to avoid it, the therapist can then propose that:

- They get out as soon as possible.
- They should remain as far as possible from the video lottery terminals or the counter where lottery tickets are sold. If they remain close to the machines, they risk seeing another gambler cash in an important win or make a substantial loss before leaving the gambling area. The result? Gamblers might think that luck is in the air and be tempted to gamble as well, or they might believe that since the other gambler lost, the machine is on the brink of paying out the jackpot.
- They should avoid asking personnel or other clients about the output of video lottery terminals, the results of lottery draws, or results of any other form of gambling game.

Finding oneself alone in a gambling establishment
For certain gamblers, the problem is not so much being in a gambling establishment as it is going alone. In fact, gamblers may regularly go to bars in the company of friends without being tempted to gamble. Even if some thoughts about gambling suddenly appear, the presence of their friends will occupy them and keep them away from danger. On the other hand, when gamblers find themselves alone in such an establishment, the likelihood that they will succumb to gambling multiplies. In this case, the therapist can suggest to gamblers that they never go to gambling places alone. Or, they can leave the establishment with the people who accompanied them, even if gamblers would rather stay a few minutes more to finish their drink. This is because the idea of gambling will surely tempt them as soon as they are alone.

Receiving an invitation to gamble

Receiving an invitation to go to a gambling establishment represents another risky situation that deserves consideration. Does the gambler find it difficult to refuse these invitations? In this case, the clinician can work with gamblers to:

- Learn to assert themselves and develop strategies to refuse such offers. In this respect, role-playing contributes to this assertiveness training: during these exercises, gamblers learn to say no, first using the therapist as a model, then playing their own role. Finally, once gamblers have well-integrated ways of rejecting invitations and are able to express their refusal, the therapist can encourage the gamblers to apply these skills to their daily interactions with others.
- Discuss their gambling problem with friends and family, telling them that the difficulty is presently being dealt with. It is also preferable that friends and family be informed that they should avoid inviting the gamblers to bars or gambling establishments if they wish to assist the gamblers in their process. Moreover, if the majority of the gamblers' friends are linked, closely or not, to their gambling activities, it is justifiable to make changes to certain relationships or to question them.

Financial situation

What is the element that contributes to the persistence of gambling habits? Obviously it is the amount of money available. That fact is undeniable and logical. The more money the gambler possesses, the more he or she risks gambling it. Consequently, in addition to avoiding exposure to gambling, we suggest that gamblers should restrict their access to money as much as possible by temporarily conferring the management of the money to a loved one or a third person, or by engaging the services of a financial consultant.

Close friends and relatives can help gamblers to better manage the incoming of money and its spending, particularly for meeting their essential needs – food, lodging, clothing – and paying their debts or other matters. Certain gamblers will find it humiliating to give control of their finances to a close friend or relative. However, other gamblers understand that, in the short run, humiliation is better than the risk of losing all.

The therapist and gambler can also discuss the possibility of requesting the services of a financial consultant or an organization to learn how to establish a budget according to his or her revenues and current expenses. The financial consultant and gambler can assess the gambler's financial situation and decide what actions to take. This financial consultant could accompany him during various procedures such as meeting a syndicate to declare bankruptcy, taking steps to consolidate loans, etc. If gamblers settle their financial situation, they will be less preoccupied by the idea of gambling to make money and will be in a better position to undergo therapy.

However, if gamblers cannot resort to one or another of these strategies, the therapist can suggest some simple means that are applicable to certain situations in order to temper their urge to gamble. Here are some probable situations and some possible solutions. If gamblers have money on hand, they should carry only a limited amount of pocket money. The therapist can also suggest that they do not keep any money with them because it could become the pretext to gamble a small amount, which may seem banal or not very serious, with the hope of making a quick win.

Gamblers who have access to money should consider the following actions:

- Canceling their credit cards
- Avoiding owning an automatic banking machine card, which allows them to pay for their purchases without manipulating money. This card, in addition to giving them easy access to money, does not allow them to see the account's balance when purchasing something. It also offers the possibility of withdrawing money in automatic banking machines, which facilitate, once more, access to money.
- Planning a limited access to their bank account, by requesting that a co-signature be required for all cash withdrawals.
- Giving clear instructions to friends, family, and owners of gambling establishments that they are not to lend the gamblers any money.

For gamblers who receive an inflow of money (salaries, wins, gift, etc.), they can:

- Ask that the cheque be automatically deposited into their bank account, to avoid having any contact with it.
- Be accompanied by a close friend or relative when depositing money into their bank account.
- Give the cheque to a spouse or a trusted person.
- Plan the payday scenario in advance: plan all of the day's activities in detail.
- Warn a friend or relative of the next arrival of money and discuss solutions.
- Give another person the responsibility of picking up the mail so as not to be in direct contact with cheques or bills received.

Lack of money is as risky a situation as is access to money. In fact, gamblers with financial difficulties become extremely preoccupied by payments to be made and debts to settle. The result is that while they may first seek real solutions to deal with the problem, gamblers may then say that, in the end, gambling remains the most rapid means of making money, even if they have lost everything. Thus, there exist several risky situations that are directly linked to a lack of financial resources, some of which are:

- Lacking money to pay for rent, food, and clothing.
- Receiving a bill.
- Having lost the evening before.
- Wanting to buy a birthday present for a loved one.
- Being invited to an outing or a leisure activity and not have enough money to participate.

How can one decrease this financial stress? Simply through communication: gamblers can speak of their gambling problem among their friends and family.

Relationship difficulties

Gamblers isolate themselves too often because of their gambling problems and, little by little, they abandon friends and family. This distance frequently establishes itself on both sides. If gamblers distance themselves because of their gambling activities and sink into their problem, family members distance themselves through exhaustion and exasperation. Over the course of therapy and during the period of recovery, gamblers learn to live with the consequences of their gambling excesses. In certain cases, they can intervene more easily, but in others, they must be patient. For several gamblers, returning to their families will not be done smoothly. It is even possible that some relationships will have completely broken off and that the climate will never be the same. Why? Because the majority of friends and family no longer trust gamblers. They have lied so often in the past to hide the extent of their gambling problems, that friends and family do not know how to distinguish true from false. Trust does not magically return. It is progressively acquired. Gamblers must expect to prove themselves. This difficult situation will often provoke feelings of discouragement, since gamblers are making efforts to cease gambling, but obtain little encouragement from most of their friends and family. Friends and family want long-term proof that the gambler can be trusted.

Often, excessive gambling leads to a deterioration of the social network. Sometimes, gamblers isolate themselves from others, while in other circumstances, friends and family distance themselves either because they have no common interests with the gambler, or because they can no longer tolerate the constant requests for money and the delays in repayment of gambling debts. In every case, excessive gambling exacerbates the isolation. Certain relationships will have definitively ended. By ceasing to gamble, gamblers will face their isolation. This loneliness constitutes another risky situation. The therapist must warn gamblers of this risk and help them to progressively resume contact with their friends.

Sometimes gamblers have a solitary personality, and the isolation brought about by gambling causes them no problem. However, gamblers may experience the need to establish relationships with others without knowing how. In bars, gamblers are surrounded by people without necessarily being in contact with them. Gambling thus provides them with a sense of community, and by ceasing to gamble, they can feel an emptiness or discomfort. What can the therapist suggest in this case? Gamblers are advised to develop a circle of friends, or, at least to begin by establishing one or two relationships. If they do not know how to develop these new relationships, the therapist could provide social skills training.

Lack of occupations and activities

Ceasing to gamble has inevitable repercussions on the course of gamblers' daily lives. All of a sudden, they have a lot of free time that they must occupy. Here are some practical suggestions. What were the gamblers' activities and interest before gambling took up all their time? Did they have passions, or hobbies? Many gamblers become aware of numerous activities that they neglected or completely abandoned as gambling became increasingly important in their lives. Certain gamblers find it relatively easy to find new pastimes and to resume their previous activities. Also, keeping oneself active avoids periods of idleness, during which gamblers are likely to be flooded with thoughts about gambling. By doing so, gamblers will notice that they manage to find satisfaction in doing things other than gambling. These activities are often less costly and are beneficial in many ways.

Other gamblers may be more passive and have always used gambling to fill a void. This emptiness can reflect a lack of relationships, but it can also manifest itself as idleness or a lack of interest in other activities. In this case, with the therapist's assistance, gamblers make a list of activities (new or otherwise) that are accessible and that are likely to interest them. We suggest they find activities they can do alone, as well as activities that require the presence of other people. Certain gamblers seek out activities involving a degree of risk or stimulation in order to feel the same adrenaline rushes that were triggered in the past by gambling. In this case, they only need to find activities that adhere to these criteria.

Which pastimes are sought out is of little importance. The important thing at this point is to fill free time in order to discover new interests, while reducing the risk of relapse. Furthermore, a part of the money that was lost to gambling will be used to cover expenses for healthier objectives with positive repercussions. Gamblers will perhaps spontaneously choose to resort to such a solution. They may, however, need assistance with this process if they do not know where to begin.

Consuming alcohol or drugs

Consuming alcohol or drugs can greatly reduce the willpower to resist gambling. Since gambling terminals are often situated in bars, the majority of people who gamble do so while drinking alcoholic beverages. It goes without saying that the effects of alcohol can impair gamblers' perceptions and prevent them from becoming aware of the seriousness of beginning or continuing to gamble. All gamblers should be warned of this danger and be encouraged to decrease their consumption of alcohol or drugs.

If the gamblers' consumption appears excessive, or that dependency is a problem, these gamblers should be referred to an appropriate resource. Sometimes, therapists treat alcohol and gambling problems conjointly, but must keep in mind that if gamblers continue to abusively consume alcohol or other substances, they impair the ability and the hindsight necessary to modify their thoughts and behaviors. Treatment in this case can be compared to a sunscreen that loses its effectiveness when the gambler dives into water. Therapy can be very useful, but in combination with alcohol a large portion of its effectiveness is removed. Gamblers lose their ability to evaluate critically. Consequently, while working on the gambling problem, gamblers will first be invited to resolve their drug or alcohol problem.

Daily problems (frustration, failure, rejection)

The lure of monetary gain and the need to escape daily difficulties are two reasons that are often invoked by gamblers to explain their gambling. The desire to gamble in order to win money is largely discussed over the course of cognitive interventions. However, certain gamblers experience difficulties that are not specific to gambling, and these can provoke relapse. How can this phenomenon be explained? An inability to deal with daily problems and a lack of problem-solving skills can lead to a desire to escape. Certain gamblers, in fact, prefer to escape difficulties rather than search for solutions. Gambling then becomes a tempting option, as it offers escape and the possibility, as minimal as it is, to win money. When this chain of events becomes apparent, the therapist must help the gamblers to find solutions. Why? Simply because we tend to repeatedly react in the same way in the face of problematic events.

The problems that we refer to here can take on diverse forms. They are difficulties or events in our daily lives, from problems that occur at work to conflictual situations at home. Clearly, we speak of any problematic situation that leads to anger, frustration, sadness, or discouragement. From the moment gamblers perceive the advantages of directly intervening in some of these difficulties, and show an inclination to do so, the therapist can teach them problem-solving steps. Summarily, these steps include:

1. *Stop and think.* Taking a pause can help to avoid reactions that are too impulsive. This pause gives the time necessary to think and resolve the problem, and to follow the other steps.
2. *Clearly identify the problem.* The therapist and gambler make a list of the main difficulties inherent to gambling problems. It is important to clearly understand the problem before knowing how to solve it. Sometimes, we know that things are going badly, or that we feel badly but we have difficulty in understanding what is going on or in identifying the problem. To help gamblers to see the problem more clearly, the therapist suggests that they ask themselves questions like: "What is happening?", "What is the problem?", "Who am I in conflict with?", etc.
3. *Define all the aspects of the situation.* In order to dissect the problem and to identify all of its aspects, the following questions can be very useful: "What don't I like about this situation?", "What exactly must change?", "What do I want or would I like?", "What is my goal?", "What are the obstacles?", "What is stopping me from attaining my goal?".
4. *List possible solutions.* Each problem can be solved in different ways. At this step, as many solutions as possible are listed without judging them or evaluating them according to their potential effectiveness. Leave room for creativity! The more we imagine solutions, the more we increase their chances of solving the problem well and overcoming the obstacles. Question such as the following will surely help the gambler: "What can I do to solve this problem?", "How could I act?", "What could I tell myself?". Be careful to avoid eliminating a solution that appears to have failed in advance! Sometimes, when seen in another light, beneficial effects can be identified.
5. *Evaluate each possibility.* For each solution, the potential consequences are examined: "What will happen if I decide to do this?", "What are the advantages of this choice?", "What are the disadvantages of this

choice?". Again, we suggest that the responses be put onto paper in order to facilitate the decision.

6. *Choose and experiment*. This is the last step. Obviously, it is logical to choose the solution that appears to be most advantageous – the one that will have positive repercussions. However, only by implementing the solution will gamblers see if it yields the expected effects and results. If the results are unsatisfactory, we suggest that they consult their list of solutions again. They could then choose another solution and experiment with it, and so on, until they reach a satisfying result.

Overall, there are no miracle or perfect solutions to any one problem. However, these steps provide a model to follow and can help gamblers to solve difficulties when they occur. At first, gamblers will need to familiarize themselves with this way of proceeding. Later, gamblers will notice that the more they repeat the same steps, the less time the problem-solving process will take. These steps will allow them to stop and think about their situation, and to make good decisions.

Finally, here is a list of ways that can help gamblers to attain or maintain abstinence from gambling:

- Participate in self-help groups like Gamblers Anonymous (GA). Meeting with other individuals who experience the same problem, and sharing with them, can help gamblers to cease gambling or maintain abstinence. Gamblers will find support and encouragement among people who have experienced the same difficulties. There are many GA groups. Since these are group meetings, it may be that certain gamblers do not feel at ease within a particular group. We thus suggest that they visit a few groups before concluding that this type of resource is not for them. This type of mutual support truly might not be suitable for some gamblers (for instance, those who are not at ease in groups or who do not adhere to the philosophy conveyed by GA). Nonetheless, this resource can be very helpful for many gamblers.
- Keep a photo of somebody they love with them and look at it when the urge to gamble occurs. The photograph is not to be used to bring luck, but rather to break the desire to gamble out of respect and love for this person.
- Plan activities in advance to remove the urge to gamble.
- Avoid free time by efficiently managing their use of time.
- Try new and stimulating activities.
- Return to activities they enjoyed before taking up gambling.
- Spend money on other leisure activities.
- Identify concrete goals (short-, mid-, and long-term goals) that they wish to attain.

- Write a motivating sentence on a small card, e.g., "Take care of you", "Do not gamble", "Gambling can only cause problems", "My choice is happiness within my family".

In conclusion, there are many spheres in which to behaviorally intervene and the proposed strategies are numerous. Behavioral strategies, used in conjunction with the correction of erroneous thoughts with regards to gambling, increase the effectiveness of the intervention and allow the gambler to attain and maintain abstinence from gambling. These two approaches effectively complement one another and address gambling problems from the maximum number of possible angles.

7

RELAPSE PREVENTION

Once gamblers have attained complete abstinence from gambling, they face another great challenge: maintaining abstinence. This challenge is considerable because abstinence results in frustration. It denies gamblers their previous sources of gratification and preferred means of escape. Realizing the actual consequences of excessive gambling thus requires a strong dose of determination and renunciation of past ideas and activities. Before, the gambler lived in his or her world of beliefs and dreams. In a difficult financial situation gamblers would say to themselves, "No problem, I can solve it in less than three hands of Blackjack." But, if gamblers strive for abstinence, they must admit to having been defeated by gambling and cease to consider it as a short-term solution to various problems. The result is that gamblers find themselves grappling with an austere financial situation, perhaps for several years. This perspective alone is enough to discourage many gamblers from trying to remain abstinent from gambling. Thus, this chapter addresses relapse prevention. First, a brief portrait of a relapse will be presented. Next, relapse will be defined and therapeutic strategies that will help gamblers to prevent it will be described. Finally, emergency measures to be put into place should relapse occur will be identified.

Portrait of a relapse

Daniel has gambled on video lottery terminals for the last three years. During his third year of gambling, he lost great sums of money. On several occasions, he spent the equivalent of one week's salary in a single evening. A difficult financial situation and a strong pressure for Daniel to quit gambling followed. He thus made the decision to stop gambling, much to the relief of everyone around him. A period of one month of abstinence went by wherein Daniel did not gamble. The situation stopped deteriorating. Daniel and his family were in the process of trying to solve financial problems.

However, one day, after having completed an important project at work, his colleagues organized a Happy Hour outing to celebrate. For the past month, Daniel had not gone to bars, knowing full well that it would be difficult for him to abstain from gambling if he were near a video lottery terminal. The bar his colleagues chose was close to the office and was the same bar where Daniel had been in the habit of gambling. However, he joined his colleagues, believing himself capable of resisting any urge to gamble. Furthermore, since none of his work companions were aware of his gambling problems, Daniel preferred to not say anything and to accompany them to the bar.

Entering the bar made a strange impression on Daniel. From time to time he anxiously glanced towards the machines. On his way to the bar to order a beer, walked near the machines, and stopped a few minutes to watch the two people playing them. The result was that his desire to gamble increased, even though he did not yet want to admit it. Then he thought, he could gamble only $10 without anyone knowing and without it having any real consequence. It was so accessible and so tempting. Thus, at seven o'clock, while his colleagues were leaving the bar, Daniel decided to go back in for a "few minutes". The process was set in motion: he put $10 into the video lottery terminal and, after ten minutes, he had already lost it. An irresistible desire to continue gambling in order to try to recuperate his $10 and to possibly win a little more seized him. In the end, he gambled for four hours and lost $140, a sum that he obviously could not afford to lose.

Still in shock, there was nothing left to do but to return home. It was a brutal return to reality. He felt disappointed and angry, as he does every time he gambles. He has difficulty understanding how he was tricked into gambling once again.

Definition of relapse

Given its many facets, relapse is defined a number of ways. For some, a relapse means a return to old gambling habits. For others, gambling upon only one occasion corresponds to relapse. According to us, relapse is a return to a gambling cycle or a loss of control in a gambling situation. However, keep in mind that relapse is temporary. This means that it can be viewed as an integral part of a normal recovery process. In fact, managing to extricate oneself from a gambling problem is rarely an instant process. Mountain climbers also sometimes slip and the climb can be difficult, but if they keep their objective in mind and persevere, they will reach the summit.

Relapse prevention integrated into therapy

Remaining under the impression that they are working only towards the objectives of honoring their financial obligations and finding new ways of dealing with their problems are gamblers' major obstacles to maintaining abstinence. Since relapse represents the greatest difficulty for therapists working in the field of dependencies, treatment that takes this glaring reality into account has to be developed. Prevention of a gambling relapse cannot be reduced to a supplementary element to be addressed at the end of treatment. Relapse prevention needs to be addressed throughout the entire therapeutic process. Thus, we are proposing a therapy in which interventions are directly linked to relapse prevention.

Beginning with the first step in treatment, the exercise concerning gamblers' destructive passion for gambling raises their awareness of this eventual slip and provides them with the means to deal with it. When therapists speak of this passion to gamblers, they encourage them to look to previous sources of pleasure or to seek out new ones, so as to quickly develop alternative behaviors. Gamblers then no longer perceive themselves as prisoners of an exclusive source of satisfaction. They get in touch with a part of themselves that they had left behind. In doing so, the notion of choice opens up to them, as does their hope of recovering control.

Before providing hope for perfect control over their gambling habits, gamblers are invited to explore their motivation to attain abstinence from gambling. They examine both the positives and negatives of choosing to continue to gamble. By listing the disadvantages, gamblers inevitably identify risky situations. For example, a gambler who is conscious of the fact that gambling will no longer be available to help manage his or her anger, must develop new strategies to resolve this difficulty. This work on motivation thus offers a wonderful opportunity to prevent relapse.

Generally, abstinence is achieved gradually. Consequently, it is essential to discuss the eventuality of relapse throughout therapy. Gamblers are informed that relapse can even be useful for many people. In fact, rather than perceive relapse as a catastrophe or failure, gamblers can use it to their advantage by consolidating their gains and identifying the erroneous thoughts that pushed them to gamble again. This is where the relevance of modifying dream-selling thoughts becomes apparent.

"Let's play" is an exercise that allows gamblers to modify their inner dialogue and to make them more aware of their life choices. We advise gamblers to use this tool every time they are tempted to gamble. Those who frequently practice this exercise immunize themselves against old automatic thoughts and increase control over their lives in general.

Once gamblers have mastered their thoughts and behavior through the use of the exercises addressed in therapy, and are ready to terminate treatment, the therapist provides emergency measures to guide them in case they experience a strong return to excessive gambling. To do so, the therapist asks gamblers to describe what relapse means for them and to identify what events, thoughts, or situations risk setting a gambling cycle into motion.

Clearly, the therapist attempts to bring out any information that is likely to help the gamblers to detect events and thoughts that are likely to trick them. Some examples of relapse situations are presented here in the form of case illustrations.

Peter's example:

RISKY SITUATION: Peter receives three expensive bills in the mail that must soon be paid. The problem is that he knows he does not have enough money to pay them.

THOUGHT: He asks himself where he will find the money to pay what he owes.

EMOTION: He feels anxious and tense.

THOUGHT: He tells himself that by gambling, he could win a small amount of money and thus be able to make his payments.

CONSEQUENCE: Peter gambles and is caught in the excessive gambling spiral.

Clara's example:

RISKY SITUATION #1: Clara has a fight at home. She leaves, slamming the door behind her.

EMOTION: She feels badly, wanting to unwind and forget everything.

RISKY SITUATION #2: She goes to a bar to have a drink. While observing the people playing video lotteries, she notices that someone has just won $250.

THOUGHT: She tells herself that the machines are paying out this evening. She thinks she deserves to win too.

CONSEQUENCE: Clara decides to bet $20.

THOUGHT: She is persuaded that she will be able to control herself.

CONSEQUENCE: Clara is caught in the excessive gambling spiral.

In order to arm gamblers with a sense of control over a massive return to gambling, the therapist questions them about their previous relapses.

- How did the gambler approach them?
- What exactly happened?
- How did the gambler resolve them?

This questioning forces gamblers to draw from their personal resources and turns them towards what they already know. By recalling the times when they knew how to control themselves, they increase their self-esteem and level of expectations. They begin to believe in their self-efficacy. Confidence and self-esteem are truly the best protection gamblers have against the often very strong temptation to gamble again.

Other actions can be integrated into the relapse prevention process.

- *Favor a gradual end to therapy.* Gradually terminating therapy assures gamblers of assistance in the case of relapse. This strategy also facilitates gamblers' adaptation to the severing of the therapeutic alliance. The process of gradually ending therapy simply involves spacing the last sessions. For example, a therapist can choose to see gamblers every two weeks, then every three weeks and, finally, once per month if necessary. Then, the therapist immediately plans a follow-up. This process provides gamblers with an anchor, reassures them, and helps to maintain their determination not to gamble, because they know that they will have to tell the therapist what has happened since their last meeting.
- *Encourage gamblers to complete their exercises.* We know that when gamblers experience a period of relapse, they stop, unfortunately, completing their exercises on the questioning of automatic thoughts. The sunscreen example helps gamblers to understand that a solution does not work if it is only applied once. For the sunscreen to be effective, it must be applied each time one exposes oneself to the sun. One application is not enough. The gamblers are thus asked to use their "Let's play" exercises each time the desire to gamble presents itself. It serves as a protective tool against their erroneous thoughts.
- *Encourage recourse to available resources and evaluate them.* This is an exercise that ensures positive results. Gamblers begin by asking themselves the following questions. Who can help me? What resources are available in my environment? They then make a list and keep it close by. Thanks to this exercise, gamblers realize that they are not alone and can obtain assistance if their desire to gamble is too insistent.
- *Promote access to mutual-aid groups.* For some gamblers, mutual-aid groups such as Gamblers Anonymous (GA) contribute to the maintenance of abstinence. Within these groups, each gambler is paired with a "sponsor", to whom he or she can resort if relapse is imminent. Moreover, pressure from the group and the solidarity in its members' determination not to gamble can keep some gamblers' momentum in check. There is strength in unity. In fact, all of the resources that are likely to help gamblers should be identified and the therapist should

encourage gamblers to consider them while working on maintaining abstinence.

Emergency measures

As a tool in case of an emergency, we use a document that is actually an adaptation of a text written by Professor Marlatt concerning the prevention of relapse to the use of alcohol. The therapist and gambler discuss the contents of this text, and the therapist recommends that he or she keep it as a memory aid.

Stop, observe and listen

If you suddenly have the urge to gamble or if you have gambled, stop for a moment. Observe and listen to what is happening inside of you. This urge to gamble or this period of gambling is warning you that you are in danger. Compare your gambling situation to a flat tire. What does a driver do when he or she has a flat tire? The first thing to do is stop on the side of the road as soon as possible in order to be safe. Then, the driver consults his or her manual or carries out a series of emergency measures to deal with the problem. If you have the urge to gamble or if you have gambled, stop and find a quiet place where you will be less distracted by this temptation. Once you have stopped, consult your "emergency measures" sheets. On these sheets, you will find specific instructions you can follow to avoid relapse. The emergency measures are:

1. Remain calm
Your first reaction to the desire to gamble might be to feel guilty or to blame yourself. Don't panic! It is normal to feel the urge to gamble. Don't forget that there is no danger except if, obviously, you decide to follow up on this desire and lose all control. So, be lucid but do not dramatize everything.

Give yourself enough time for the desire to gamble to fade. The urge to gamble is like an ocean wave: it rises, crashes down, pushes forward, and then recedes. If you do not give in when it presents itself, it will probably disappear as it came.

Avoid negatively evaluating yourself. Simply play the role of an observer and calmly wait for the urge to pass. Distance yourself from what is happening to you because, in addition to being pointless, self-depreciation can only work against you.

Whatever happens, try not to give into desires that risk reactivating your old habits. Remember that your automatic thoughts will invite you to gamble again, but that you have the power to modify them.

If, despite everything, you give into your urge to gamble, it will surely be even more difficult to control yourself. But above all, do not forget this: gambling again should not be considered as a total failure. If you slip and fall on a patch of ice, does that mean that you have to learn how to walk again? Do not conclude that gambling one more time makes you a person without willpower who will surely fail. That is not so! Rather it is a unique and independent event that you can avoid in the future. We learn from our mistakes.

2. *Remember your commitment*
After gambling again, your motivation and your control become fragile. You might want to abandon everything and believe that you completely failed. Again, this is a normal reaction. Here are some tricks that will help during these difficult moments:

- Think again about the reasons why you decided to stop gambling. Consult the exercise that let you determine the advantages and disadvantages of gambling and ceasing to gamble. Then review the situation. What long-term "gains" does abstinence from gambling provide you with? You are not going to renounce them under the pretext that you had some difficulty.
- Talk to yourself and contrast your contradictions: in the left corner, the side of you that wants to stop gambling, and in the right corner, the side of you that wants to drop your weapons and abandon everything. Remember that it was, first and foremost, for yourself that you decided to change your habits, in order to take care of yourself and your life.
- Look back and see all the efforts you invested into this change and the progress you have made. Be optimistic rather than fixate on your current difficulties. Think about all the times you had the urge to gamble and you were able to resist. What would most help you to abstain from gambling?
- Do you truly believe that one sole relapse cancels all the progress you've made up until now? Remember your commitment and long-term goals. Don't forget: you have control over your actions and you are the master of your destiny.

3. *Carefully analyze the situation*
Never give into the reflex of making yourself feel guilty, because it will be even more difficult to effectively act afterwards. Ask yourself questions. Interrogate yourself about the context, the time of day, the presence or

absence of people, your mood or your activities at the moment when the urge to gamble was at its worst and, above all, the thoughts that trigger and promote this urge to gamble. Remember that risky situations generate thoughts that lead towards gambling if the gambler does not confront them. What thoughts provoked the relapse? Were there warning signs before the relapse? What was the risky situation? Each of these questions can provide precious information and allow you to sharpen your vigilance against urges to gamble.

If relapses occur frequently, that means that something is happening and that you should attend to it. Did you try to do something before the relapse occurred? If yes, what strategy did you use to thwart your urge to gamble? Why did it turn out to be ineffective? What could you do next time in order to act more effectively upon this situation? If you did nothing, why did you react that way? Was your motivation weakened? Why?

Imagine that the scenario has recurred. See yourself as strong and able to react effectively. Go over, in your mind, all the methods you know to prevent yourself from giving into the temptation. Replace inadequate thoughts you have about gambling, or about maintaining your urge to gamble, with thoughts that are more adequate. Never forget that you have control over your thoughts and behavior.

4. Ask for help
If you feel that, after several individual attempts, you are still unable to identify what could have provoked your relapse, do not hesitate to ask for help, whether it is from your friends, a support organization, or a therapist. Phone and clearly state that you need help. The driver who has a flat tire and who is unable to deal with the situation alone does not hesitate to wave down a passing car or to call a mechanic. Do like this wise driver and allow yourself to ask for help…

Memory aid

In case of relapse:

1. Stay calm, distance myself and think about what just happened.
2. Identify the thoughts that led me to gamble.
3. Examine my conviction of winning and remember the principles of chance:
   - the result is unpredictable
   - each turn is new
   - no strategy is possible, no control over the outcome of a game
   - negative expectancy: more to lose than to win.
   - winning conviction is a lure

4. Remember all the efforts I have made until now.
5. Remember all the advantages of stopping gambling.
6. Ask for help if the preceding steps fail.

Relapse prevention is a very important aspect of the therapy, as relapse is a great enemy for one who wishes to stop gambling. Not giving in to the temptation to gamble again is truly a sizeable challenge. However, by having these tools on hand, gamblers are ready to face the many opportunities to gamble that will inevitably mark their route.

8

DIFFICULTIES RELATED TO THE TREATMENT: HOW TO OVERCOME THEM

All therapists are well aware that clinical reality is more difficult or different than what one anticipates. The treatment of excessive gambling is no exception. Some situations or behaviors can be disconcerting to the therapist. For example, what can be done if a gambler asserts that chance does not exist or that he or she is receiving threats from a loan shark? One thing is certain: the list of difficulties that can arise in therapy is infinite. In this chapter we present some of these difficulties for which we propose some clinical tips.

There is no such thing as chance

The main component of treatment is based on a better understanding of chance. Gamblers misunderstand chance and often confound games of chance with games of skill. As mentioned previously, the therapist and gambler must agree on a definition of chance. The majority of gamblers will define chance as an uncontrollable and unpredictable phenomenon. However, the therapist may sometimes meet gamblers who confidently assert that chance does not exist. What can be done in such a situation?

First, the therapist can ask these gamblers to explain what they mean exactly by this assertion. Some gamblers will assert that life is programmed in advance. They believe that chance is akin to destiny, that everything is already planned, and one can do nothing to change the course or outcome of events. Others will define chance from a more philosophical point of view. According to these determinists, all events have a reason for being and everything happens for a reason. Some gamblers will also allude to premonitions, luck, and feelings. Others will defend the idea that chance is a probability and that one can predict events with clever calculations.

It is not advisable to confront such gamblers on their ideas about chance. However, it is still necessary to agree on a more basic definition of this concept. Any definition of chance must involve the notions of unpredictability and absence of control. Here is an example in which a therapist helps a gambler to accept and understand the definition used in therapy.

THERAPIST: You're telling me that there is no such thing as chance. What exactly do you mean by that?

GAMBLER: What I mean is that I don't believe that the things that happen to us are by chance. You know, there are people who are luckier than others, people who have something special. It is not chance or an accident that some people win more often. There are people who can feel things. Things never happen for no reason.

THERAPIST: You seem to have thought about this question a lot and your view of chance is quite philosophical. What we mean here by chance in gambling games could be directly taken out of a dictionary. If I asked you to explain what chance is to a young child, what would be your explanation?

GAMBLER: I would say that it is something that happens and that we can't plan it. We can't know if it will happen or at what moment it will occur. And regardless of what we do, it will happen, it happens...

THERAPIST: So, chance is something that we can't plan, and on which our actions have no impact, since what must happen happens. Do you agree with this definition?

GAMBLER: Yes, it's pretty much that. It's quite a simple and narrow definition, but it can also be that.

This method of insisting on a dictionary definition has the advantage of not frustrating gamblers and often helps them to dissociate chance from notions of destiny, luck, and even premonitions. This approach does not involve denying that premonitions and destiny are part of some people's realities, but simply to spread doubt as to their efficacy when it comes to games of chance. Such an approach also avoids interminable discussions about the true definition of chance.

To sum up, because the proper course of treatment rests on a correct understanding of chance, it is very important that gamblers and therapists agree upon its definition. It is pointless to confront gamblers on their vision of chance. We may have to be satisfied with a mutually agreed upon, simple, and operational definition of chance that is based on the fact that one can neither predict nor control it. While it is preferable that this understanding be reached at the beginning of therapy, this idea can occasionally be put aside and addressed later in the process.

The gambler persists in viewing games of chance as games of skill

Despite all the information and explanations that the therapist can provide to gamblers regarding the uncontrollable and unpredictable nature of games of chance, sometimes gamblers persist in viewing games of chance as games of skill.

It is now known that commercially exploited games of chance are chosen on the grounds of two very precise characteristics: (1) that it is impossible for a person to predict the result of the next game and (2) that no skill is required to play.

Unfortunately, stories still circulate that maintain false beliefs in the possibility to master certain games of chance. Many books and magazines exist that perpetuate these myths and maintain these illusions of control. For example, some gamblers may say that casinos regularly exclude Blackjack gamblers because they are winning too much or counting cards.

We believe it is essential to remain skeptical about these claims. Some may be true, while others are clearly mythical. It is quite possible that expelled gamblers, a very rare phenomenon, are part of an underground network working within casinos. The result is that gamblers cling to these stories and to the idea that there is a way to control chance. They wish to get the better of chance. They want to be the big winner!

Admittedly, while chance plays a large part in the outcome of many card games, gamblers' skill and experience effectively increase their chances of winning at certain card games. Bridge players, for example, use strategies and make deductions to better stand up against an opponent. And, when playing poker between friends, knowing how to bluff can be very useful. In this type of game, it is thus possible to improve and it is not illusory to believe in one's skill. But we must be careful! Casinos are well aware of this reality and do not take any risks. They systematically eliminate any kind of game where skill can make the results lean in favor of the gamblers.

Moreover, while games of chance offer no opportunity for financial return in the long run, nothing prevents gamblers from proceeding in a way that limits their losses. For example, in Blackjack, the only skill required consists of obeying certain basic rules in order to lose less in the long run. But, beyond obeying these rules, gamblers can in no way increase their chances of winning. Conversely, disobeying these rules results in an increase in the probabilities of losses in the long run.

In Blackjack and other card games, gamblers often fantasize about eventually being able to count cards like "professional" gamblers who make their living thanks to this rare talent. This is a lovely myth. If we consider the reality imposed by a return rate that is less than 100%, it is absolutely impossible for a person who repeatedly plays to come out a winner. And although Blackjack offers a very high return rate, approximately 99%, it still remains inferior to 100%.

Some gamblers claim that by counting cards, it becomes possible to increase their return, which would allow them to have an advantage over the casino. But this improvement in their return is not conceivable unless one plays with only one deck of cards. In casinos, three, five or even six decks of cards are used within a single shoe, which is surely to the casino owner's advantage.

Let us take a look at the numbers. Consider a person who perfectly counts cards and who asserts having a 0.5% advantage over the casino. In the best of cases, if this person bets $100 each hand, he or she wins, on average, $0.05 per hand. Thus, if he or she plays 60 hands at $100 ($6,000), he or she will have won $30. What purpose does it serve to risk $6,000 for the possibility – not certainty – of winning $30? It's insane. Furthermore, these "professional gamblers", these living myths, advise you to have 300 times your average bet in your pocket in order to face variations in potential losses. But the probabilities have been established over a long period of time. Gamblers could very well win their first two bets and then lose the next 20. This proves that, even by counting cards, it is impossible to predict with certainty which card the dealer will turn up. Let us also add that at the beginning of a deck, the dealer asks a gambler to cut the shoe with a colored plastic card, which the dealer then uses to indicate the end of the shoe. Consequently, certain cards will never be revealed. How can one guess which cards? It is impossible! The structure of the game prevents anyone from winning in the long run. So, regardless of which strategy is used, the only law that prevails is the law of chance.

However, gamblers have difficulty admitting that they have no impact on the game's result. Over the years, they have often developed a great number of strategies that they believe will help them to play better and gain an advantage. This is a huge deception. Thus it is normal, even predictable, that many gamblers are depressed and self-deprecating when they learn this bad news. How could I have been so "stupid" all these years?, they ask themselves. The therapist's job is to reassure. He or she can explain that, before therapy, gamblers did not know the traps of gambling games. Consequently, it was difficult for them to resist these traps. The traps are brilliantly orchestrated. Moreover, at that time, gamblers simply did not possess the knowledge needed to face them. The therapist can help discouraged gamblers see that it is not their lack of intelligence, but rather a lack of information, that greatly limited their freedom of choice.

This phenomenon repeats itself among horse race and sports betting amateurs. At the racetrack or in the betting parlor, one can find many "connoisseur" bettors who apparently have been tipped off and know the horses on which to bet. Nonetheless, it should be mentioned here that research has demonstrated that an inexperienced bettor will lose as much as the most specialized bettor. The reason is simple: the rate of return at horse races is also less than 100%. Let us cite what is clearly specified in a race track's rules: "The race track acts as a stock market firm, deducting a fixed percentage of the wagers made, regardless of the finish-line results. Winning bettors share the bets once the taxes and administrations fees are deducted."

It should also be noted that the more often a horse is chosen, the less return there is for a winning bet made on it. Moreover, the amount won after a race depends on the total sum of money that was bet by all bettors. Additionally, simple bets (one horse or one race) offer a smaller return than combined bets (two horses or more and several races). The same rule prevails for betting in other sports: the more probable the result, the smaller the win. Finally, who can predict whether a horse might trip and bring down the horse that we predicted would place first? It is impossible for anyone to know which horse will win. The same applies to other sports betting: how can one predict the injury or blunders of a star player?

In sum, there are so many parameters that determine the course of a race or sports game that it is absolutely impossible to predict the result. Only one thing is certain: the more a person bets, the more he or she loses. As in all games of chance, the gambling industry ensures that, in total, it will return less money to the bettors than the amount they bet.

Believing in the idea of control: "Just $20..."

We are still not able to say whether it is possible for a person suffering from an excessive gambling problem to be able at some future time, to gamble in a controlled fashion. However, we can assert without a doubt, that one of the biggest illusions that gamblers can entertain is the belief that they can gamble "just $20.00...", convincing themselves that they will be able to restrain themselves from going any farther. Many gamblers begin therapy with the by now familiar phrase: "I told myself that I would just gamble $20, that it wouldn't do any harm! But I lost it quickly, and then I bet another $20, then $40..."

Gamblers must learn to be on their guard and admit that, if they decide to play their famous $20, they greatly risk being swept away and spending a lot more. In fact, their experience has proven it to them several times. Eventually, they will come to understand that the idea of gambling only $20 is one of the justifications they invent to give themselves "permission" to gamble. They must beware of these dangerous ideas that make them lose control and push them to gamble again.

GAMBLER: I told myself that I would just wager $20, calmly, and that I had the means to risk $20. I figured could stop myself once they were spent. I thought that it wouldn't do any harm.

THERAPIST: Let's write down what you said and look at each of these ideas. You said that you would just gamble $20 calmly. This idea thus encouraged you to gamble. With your experience as a gambler and the knowledge you have acquired up until now, what could you tell yourself in order to decrease your desire to gamble?

GAMBLER: I could tell myself that I have never just wagered $20! That amount is so quickly spent. Also, I'm not able to gamble calmly. When I lose, I accelerate the rhythm and I don't relax at all. I become extremely stressed and I dive my hands back into my pockets to find more money to bet...

THERAPIST: Excellent! You should look reality in the face and beware of the idea that you can calmly gamble only $20, which has but one role: to encourage you to gamble again. It is your lion that is trying to take control. So you should modify this idea in order for it to go in the direction you wish: to not gamble! Let's now look at the second idea: "I have the means to risk $20 and I figured could stop myself once it was spent."

GAMBLER: I could tell myself that I do not have the means to lose $20 because I know full well that if I'm going to gamble, I'll spend a lot more. That would be very harmful to me. If I do so, I will no longer have enough money to gamble at all. I'm unable to control myself once I start gambling. I go crazy! So I'm telling myself lies when I tell myself that I'll be able to stop after having spent only $20...

Thanks to this kind of exercise, gamblers understand that they have the power to control their thoughts and actions, and that they can modify them. They become aware of the automatic thoughts that lead them to gamble, while learning at the same time how to modify them with the assistance of acquired knowledge and their willingness to cease gambling. If gamblers practice this type of exercise, they will become stronger, and masters of their destiny. When a risky situation presents itself, they will be better able to resist their desire to gamble.

I gamble because gambling brings me excitement

Some gamblers compare gambling to the consumption of drugs. Gambling provides them with excitement that no other activity can offer them. Certain gamblers will mention physical withdrawal sensations when they are craving or when it is impossible for them to gamble. Accordingly, these people suffer a lot when ceasing their gambling activities.

When gamblers experience a serious gambling problem, this state of excitement tends to decrease as they continue to gamble and forces them to increase the dose. Like the alcoholic or drug addict, gamblers progressively need to wager more and more in order to attain their desired degree of excitement. A win that brought great pleasure at the beginning eventually becomes only meager relief for people who gamble excessively. Accordingly, a loss that qualified as considerable at the beginning, becomes minimal with time and no longer provokes the same feelings.

Remembering the experience of powerful excitement is one of the thoughts that incite gamblers to gamble. The promise of strong sensations provides a good reason to gamble. Gamblers might also believe that nothing can produce the powerful sensations that gambling does, and that only gambling allows them to forget everything. Their thoughts orient themselves towards what seems positive about gambling, rather than the negative consequences of gambling. The gamblers' thoughts set up traps, but nothing really prevents them from taking back control. But how can this be accomplished?

It is not necessary to attack the gambler's perception directly. However, the therapist can sow seeds of doubt in the gambler's mind. Asking gamblers to observe themselves carefully before and during gambling sessions is a very effective method. What is the intensity of their pleasure and how does it vary over the course of the session? The gamblers will probably discover that they do not experience as much pleasure as they thought. The anticipated pleasure never equals the actual pleasure experienced when gambling. They will notice that they find gambling pleasurable only when they win. When they think about it, they may notice that they feel more relieved than triumphant when they win. This personal realization often carries more weight for gamblers than a therapist's observation.

Unwavering ideas

In general, when gamblers stubbornly maintain an idea, it is useless to convince them otherwise. Take the example of the gambler who is convinced that he or she will stop gambling after just one more win. For the moment, they are always losing, but they firmly believe that they will cease gambling when they win. The therapist may try desperately to get them to see that, even if they were to win, all of their false hopes would rise to the surface again and their sole desire would be to gamble more. However, the gamblers are certain to stick to their ideas for as long as they refuse to confront reality. The therapist can thus suggest to these gamblers to make systematic observations or even to take a break in treatment in order to test their hypothesis. Such an exercise wastes the time of neither the therapist nor the gamblers and, in the future, can help them avoid discussions that lead nowhere.

It is also possible that gamblers will find the treatment simplistic and claim that their problem has deeper roots than the therapist thinks. In this case, it should be clearly reiterated that this therapy is interested in the factors that maintain gambling habits rather than their causes. Because, most importantly, the gambling behavior must end for the person to recover control over his or her life. It is necessary that people cease gambling before they can recover control of their lives. The example of a house on fire well illustrates this assertion.

THERAPIST: I understand very well that your gambling problem has deep causes and that it's important for you to get to the source of the problem. However, I would nonetheless like to make a comparison. Your current situation resembles a house in flames. Everything is burning: the financial situation, family, work, the stress that's eating you up, etc.

GAMBLER: Yeah … it looks like that.

THERAPIST: What is the first thing to do in case of a fire?

GAMBLER: Leave the house as quickly as possible.

THERAPIST: And then?

GAMBLER: Call the fire department so that that they'll put out the fire!

THERAPIST: Exactly. That's the most logical thing to do. The therapy that I'm offering here aims to help you get out of your house and put out the fire. Then we can explore the causes of the blaze. We can't explore the causes while the fire is burning. So I'm suggesting that we proceed by steps. The first step consists of working towards the cessation of gambling behavior, so that your life stops burning up. Then, you can take the time to explore causes and really get to the bottom of things. Does that proposition suit you? Think about it carefully and then make your decision.

With this attitude, we respect gamblers while explaining our way of conducting therapy. Moreover, we often notice that the action that perpetuates gambling behavior is not the one that triggers it. To slow the gambling problem, the issues that maintain gambling habits must first be attacked. Erroneous ideas about gambling assuredly are the most important maintaining factor. Belief in the possibility of recuperating losses, gambling only $20, relaxing by gambling, and forgetting problems are some of the many ideas that encourage people to gamble.

However, if the gambler still insists in finding in-depth and unconscious causes of his or her gambling problems, the therapist has two options: if the therapist feels able to do it, he or she can accompany the gambler in this process. If not, he or she can refer the gambler to another therapist who works in this perspective.

Tardiness, absences, and missed appointments

What leads gamblers to arrive late for their appointments, to miss them or to reschedule them? There are many reasons. These behaviors often reflect the gamblers' ambivalence regarding their decision to cease gambling.

This question should be clearly addressed in therapy. Gamblers should be told that their reactions are normal. By warning gamblers of these possibilities, they will perhaps be less tempted to lie or to invent all sorts of reasons to explain their absences or tardiness.

Here are some of the motives for rescheduling or canceling appointments:

- *Lack of money.* The gambler may not be able to pay for his or her session.
- *A relapse.* The gambler may feel guilty towards his or her therapist. The gambler may think that he or she has betrayed the therapist's confidence and prefer to avoid the meeting, and feels ashamed to admit to having faltered.
- *Loss of confidence.* A relapse erodes gamblers' self-confidence. As a result, they may believe themselves unable to cease gambling and tell themselves that it is not worth continuing therapy.
- *Doubt about the therapeutic process.* A relapse can weaken belief in the benefits of therapy. Gamblers may think that the therapy is ineffective because they relapsed.

The therapist should come to an understanding with gamblers at the beginning of therapy. They should agree on what are acceptable and unacceptable excuses for being late or absent from appointments. Most importantly, the therapist should warn gamblers that lateness and absences are situations that are likely to occur and to agree on this issue.

Lying during therapy

Lying is one of the diagnostic criteria for excessive gambling. It is an obvious symptom. Therapists can only work with the material that gamblers wish to share. Of course, the therapist might speak with other people sharing the gambler's life, with his or her permission. However, a relationship must first develop between the gambler and the therapist. It is important to have an open attitude with gamblers, and to avoid all forms of moralization. A condescending attitude could lead gamblers to hide certain things because they do not want the therapist to lecture them or to perceive them negatively.

Gamblers and their therapists form a team with a common goal: for the gambler to quit gambling. It is to the gambler's advantage to be frank with the therapist. The therapist may provide some examples of situations that may lead gamblers to lie over the course of therapy. Gamblers may lie:

- to minimize the seriousness of the gambling problem;
- to please the therapist;
- to make the therapist believe that the situation is improving;
- because they are tired of coming to therapy and saying they have gambled again;
- because it is embarrassing or fearful for them to admit having committed illegal acts;
- because it is embarrassing for them to say they spent 12 hours gambling on the same machine that devoured $900;
- because they need to succeed in therapy, such as in the case of a court order;
- to explain why they were late for, or absent from, an appointment.

The therapist can never be certain of the veracity of gamblers' assertions. Nonetheless, the therapist will use whatever elements gamblers wish to reveal and help them to the best of his or her ability. Such are the limits of the therapeutic relationship.

Lack of cooperation

Over the course of therapy, gamblers are the drivers of change. They are the principal actors. They are asked to invest as much energy between meetings as during therapy sessions. Some will say that they do not like filling out self-observation forms or that they do not have enough time to complete the proposed exercises.

Together with the therapist, gamblers will discover the reasons why they do not want to practice these exercises. What do the exercises represent for them? What do they not like about the exercises? It is possible that didactic work may not suit those who do not write very well, while others would rather write in a journal. It is important to be creative while remaining focused on cognitions.

Depression and suicidal ideation

Obviously, if gamblers show severe signs of depression or suicidal thoughts, these problems should be treated as priorities. No risks should be taken with a person who is very depressed or suicidal. First, the therapist must ensure that the gambler knows whom to turn to or where to go to if intense suicidal ideas surface. The therapist can also make a life contract with the gambler. Depending on the situation, it might be appropriate to suggest that the gambler consult a doctor and to obtain medical or pharmacological monitoring. It is essential to see to the gambler's safety. The therapist and gambler can return to therapy once the situation has stabilized.

Financial issues

We have already addressed the issue of finances in the section on behavior. However, here we will present two specific situations: when gamblers are being threatened by shylocks and when gamblers are requesting financial aid from friends and/or family.

When gamblers are being threatened by shylocks, they undoubtedly have very severe gambling problems. This is a particularly delicate situation as gamblers often associate with the criminal element. In light of the very real dangers that gamblers face, we, as therapists, need to realize the limitations of our interventions.

Obviously, it is very difficult to conduct therapy under such conditions. Fear of reprisals becomes a motivation for gamblers to gamble. These threats perpetuate the problem because, in order to reimburse the shylock, gamblers must find money quickly, and the only way they can make money quickly is by gambling. Obviously, one cannot easily remove oneself from such a scene.

At this stage, gamblers should not have access to money because the temptation to gamble will be too great. If they are in therapy, they should be closely monitored and a third person should manage their finances. If possible, an agreement with friends and family should be made in order to reimburse the shylock. The therapist must be aware of the traumatic nature of this aspect of gamblers' experiences because their physical integrity, or that of friends and family, is being threatened. Such threats activate survival reflexes: fight or flight. Here we suggest some solutions that may be adopted according to the situation. Remember that these gamblers find themselves in a serious situation and it is possible that the therapist will be unable to assist them.

First, the therapist can suggest that gamblers treat the shylock as a priority. Gamblers can choose to make an agreement with the shylock or try to postpone the due date of their repayments. It may be preferable for the shylock to wait longer in order to get back what is owed rather than break a gambler's legs and never recuperate the money. Do not forget that, even if gamblers file for bankruptcy, they cannot escape a shylock that is not "legal" lender.

Like victims of domestic violence, gamblers who are being threatened by a shylock might consider escape. However, there are no safe houses for gamblers. Moving or running away may be a safe solution in the short term, but it does not guarantee safety in the medium or long term. Gamblers might decide not to reimburse the shylock and assume the consequences, and only the future will tell whether their decision was wrong or right. In short, gamblers who are being threatened by a shylock are living in a very delicate situation. In such circumstances, no solutions guarantee results. Unfortunately, the shylock's pressure often surpasses the efforts put forth in therapy.

Should friends and family lend money to the gambler? Often, gamblers' friends or family contact the therapist in order to know whether or not they should lend them money. Important financial difficulties frequently push gamblers to ask friends and family to lend them money. Friends and family find themselves in difficult, even heartrending situations because they want to help the gambler to recover. But at the same time, they do not know whether lending them money is the right thing to do. Furthermore, they know very well that it is very unlikely that gamblers will be able to repay the money.

The therapist can provide advice to friends and family, but the decision of whether or not to lend the gambler money is entirely theirs. The therapist's role is to inform these people of the possible consequences of lending money, and not to decide for them.

We generally advise friends and family not to lend money to the gambler. If he or she has not yet taken responsibility for the financial consequences of his or her gambling, borrowing money is likely to minimize them. Gamblers might even decide to continue gambling if they are being lent money. We know that it is difficult for friends and family to refuse to lend money because of their emotional connection and also because gamblers are often masters in the arts of manipulation and lying. And even if gamblers truly have every intention of returning the money they borrow, their problem will drive them to gamble, even if they win. Friends and family might be afraid that gamblers will be driven to suicide if they do not overcome their financial difficulties.

Despite all, it is in the interest of the gambler's friends and family to protect themselves financially, and to ensure that the gambler does not lead them into a financial abyss. To do so, friends and family might ask a financial counselor, notary, or lawyer to assist them. Unless they have a limitless source of money, nobody can finance the practice of excessive gambling.

Stagnation of treatment

If therapy seems to plateau or to be going in circles, it is time to stop and analyze the situation. The therapist should first determine whether gamblers have the same impression and then ask them if they can explain the stagnation. Several questions may be asked in order to assess the situation:

- What progress has been made since the beginning of therapy?
- Do certain aspects of the therapy displease the gambler?
- Does the gambler have a good understanding of the concepts addressed?
- Is the gambler able to apply the new strategies?

The therapist can also question the gambler's ambivalence, review his or her therapeutic goals, and identify other activities that would help him or her to stay away from gambling.

Ignorance of the game the gambler plays

There are many different games of chance: card games, lottery, sports betting, slot machines, video lotteries, etc. Consequently, it is possible that the therapist does not know very much about the game the gambler plays. What can be done in this case? The therapist can simply admit to having limited knowledge of this game and specify that he or she would like to know more about its rules, the way it is played, the possible wins, etc. For the therapist, here is a great occasion to explore the gambler's erroneous cognitions about his or her favorite game. It is not necessary to know the particular game well to be able to detect erroneous perceptions. It is enough to be attentive to the gambler's conviction of winning, illusions of control, and tendency to make links between independent events. The therapist can thus kill two birds with one stone! He or she will learn about the game being discussed and will have within his or her grasp, many cognitions to work on.

Conclusion

We have presented some thoughts on the difficulties that can occur over the course of therapy. Based on our experience, we have suggested some solutions that may be useful in dealing with these difficulties. These clues might serve as a starting point on your search for solutions to therapeutic difficulties. We would like to end here by saying that it is better to bet on our strengths than on chance.

Appendix 1

THE SOUTH OAKS GAMBLING SCREEN*

1. Please indicate which of the following types of gambling you have done in your lifetime. For each type, mark one answer: "not at all", "less than once a week", or "once a week or more".

	Not at all	Less than once a week	Once a week or more
(a) Played cards for money.	☒	☐	☐
(b) Bet on horses, dogs, or other animals (in off-track betting, at the track, or with a bookie).	☒	☐	☐
(c) Bet on sports (parlay cards, with a bookie, or at a jai alai).	☒	☐	☐
(d) Played dice games (including craps, over and under, or other dice games) for money.	☒	☐	☐
(e) Went to a casino (legal or otherwise).	☒	☐	☐
(f) Played the numbers or bet on lotteries.	☒	☐	☐
(g) Played bingo.	☒	☐	☐
(h) Played the stock and/or commodities market.	☒	☐	☐
(i) Played slot machines, poker machines, or other gambling machines.	☒	☐	☐
(j) Bowled, shot pool, played golf, or played some other game of skill for money.	☒	☐	☐

*Copyright 1992, South Oaks Foundation; reprinted by permission. (See Henry R. Lesieur and Sheila B. Blume (1987) The South Oaks Gambling Screen (SOGS): A new instrument for the identification of pathological gamblers. *American Journal of Psychiatry*, **144** (9), 1184–1188.)

2. What is the largest amount of money you have ever gambled with on any one day ?

Never have gambled	☒	More than $100 up to $1,000	☐
$1 or less	☐	More than $1,000 up to $10,000	☐
More than $1 up to $10	☒	More than $10,000	☐
More than $10 up to $100	☐		

3. Do (did) your parents have a gambling problem ?

Both my father and mother gamble (or gambled) too much ☐
My father gambles (or gambled) too much ☐
My mother gambles (or gambled) too much ☐
Neither one gambles (or gambled) too much ☒

4. When you gamble, how often do you go back another day to win back money you lost ?

Never ☒
Some of the times (less than half the time) I lost ☐
Most of the times I lost ☐
Every time I lost ☐

5. Have you ever claimed to be winning money gambling but weren't really? In fact, you lost ?

Never (or never gamble) ☒
Yes, less than half the time I lost ☐
Yes, most of the time ☐

6. Do you feel you have ever had a problem with gambling?

No ☒
Yes, in the past, but not now ☐
Yes ☐

7. Did you ever gamble more than you intended to?

Yes ☐   No ☒

8. Have people criticized your gambling?

Yes ☐   No ☒

9. Have you ever felt guilty about the way you gamble or what happens when you gamble?

Yes ☐   No ☒

10. Have you ever felt like you would like to stop gambling but didn't think you could?

    Yes ☐   No ☒

11. Have you ever hidden betting slips, lottery tickets, gambling money or other signs of gambling from your spouse, children, or other important people in your life?

    Yes ☐   No ☒

12. Have you ever argued with people you live with over how you handle money?

    Yes ☐   No ☒

13. (If you answered "Yes" to question 12): Have money arguments ever centered on your gambling ?

    Yes ☐   No ☐

14. Have you ever borrowed from someone and not paid it back as a result of your gambling ?

    Yes ☐   No ☒

15. Have you ever lost time from work (or school) due to gambling ?

    Yes ☐   No ☒

16. If you borrowed money to gamble or to pay gambling debts, who or where did you borrow from ? (Check "Yes" or "No" for each)

    (a) From household money   Yes ☐   No ☐
    (b) From you spouse   Yes ☐   No ☐
    (c) From other relatives or in-laws   Yes ☐   No ☐
    (d) From banks, loan companies,
        or credit unions   Yes ☐   No ☐
    (e) From credit cards   Yes ☐   No ☐
    (f) From loan sharks (Shylocks)   Yes ☐   No ☐
    (g) You cashed in stocks, bonds,
        or other securities   Yes ☐   No ☐
    (h) You sold personal or family
        property   Yes ☐   No ☐
    (i) You borrowed on your checking
        account (passed bad checks)   Yes ☐   No ☐
    (j) You have (had) a credit line
        with a bookie   Yes ☐   No ☐
    (k) You have (had) a credit line
        with a casino   Yes ☐   No ☐

Scoring

Scores on the South Oaks Gambling Screen itself are determined by adding up the number of questions that show an "at risk" response:

Questions 1, 2, and 3 are not counted.
- [ ] Question 4: most of the time I lost, or every time I lost
- [ ] Question 5: yes, less than half the time I lost, or yes, most of the time
- [ ] Question 6: yes, in the past, but not now, or yes
- [ ] Question 7: yes
- [ ] Question 8: yes
- [ ] Question 9: yes
- [ ] Question 10: yes
- [ ] Question 11: yes

Question 12 is not counted.
- [ ] Question 13: yes
- [ ] Question 14: yes
- [ ] Question 15: yes
- [ ] Question 16(a): yes
- [ ] Question 16(b): yes
- [ ] Question 16(c): yes
- [ ] Question 16(d): yes
- [ ] Question 16(e): yes
- [ ] Question 16(f): yes
- [ ] Question 16(g): yes
- [ ] Question 16(h): yes
- [ ] Question 16(i): yes

Questions 16(j) and 16(k) are not counted.

Total = _____ (20 questions are counted)
5 or more = probable pathological gambler

Appendix 2

DIAGNOSTIC INTERVIEW FOR PATHOLOGICAL GAMBLING

Centre québécois d'excellence pour la prévention et le traitement du jeu
École de psychologie, Université Laval, Québec (Québec) G1K 7P4

Be empathetic. Let the person speak about his or her problem and what brings him or her here in order to create a good contact (this information can be taken up later in order to complete the interview). Try not to look like you are reading the questions, and most of all, be careful not to ask questions for which the answers have already been provided.

Gambling history

1. **(a) With regards to gambling, what led you to consult?**

    _____

    _____

    _____

    Code the responses according to the grid below:

    Court order
    Curiosity
    Already gambled compulsively (no longer gambles)
    For preventative measures
    Desire to solve gambling problem
    Other

1. **(b) Was there a particular event that prompted you to consult?**

   Do not read the choices. You can ask sub-questions up to the identification of three reasons (first reason = 1, second reason = 2, and third reason = 3).

   Yes _____   No _____

                                                    Comments

   Threat of a break-up or
   pressure from a spouse
   or partner because
   of gambling   _____   _____

   Break-up because of
   gambling   _____   _____

   Threats or pressure from
   an employer   _____   _____

   Loss of employment
   because of gambling   _____   _____

   Loss of control over
   gambling   _____   _____

   Loss of important
   material goods   _____   _____

   Other

2.

	Games played over the course of the last 12 months (see SOGS) (Yes/No)	Do you have difficulty controlling yourself when playing this game? (Yes/No)	If yes, how long ago did this difficulty begin?
A. Lotteries			

B. Casino
   Blackjack
   Roulette
   Baccarat
   Keno
   Slot-machines			

C. Bingo			
D. Cards			
E. Horse, dog, or other animal races			
F. Stock market			
G. Video lottery terminals			
H. Bowling, billiards, golf, other games of skill			
I. Dice			
J. Sports betting			

3. **You were saying that you had difficulty controlling yourself when playing (mention the games already identified in question 2) _____. During your first experiences with this/these game(s), do you remember having won a large amount?**

   It is not necessary that this question refer to their first experience, rather over the course of their first experiences.

   Yes _____   No _____

   If "Yes": How much did you win? _____

   What amount did you wager? _____

   How longer ago did that happen? _____

4. **During your childhood (0–12 years old) or adolescence (13–18 years old), did you play arcade games (pinball, Pacman, etc.) or video games like Nintendo, etc.?**

   Here, the game played is not important; we wish to verify whether the person played electronic, arcade, and video games, or any other game that falls within this category.

   Yes _____   No _____

   If "Yes": During your childhood (0–12 years), how much time did you generally spend playing these games?

   Read all the choices

0	1	2	3	4	5
No time at all	Very little time	A little time	A moderate amount of time	A lot of time	A tremendous amount of time

   And during your adolescence (13–18 years), how much time did you spend playing these games?

   Read all the choices

0	1	2	3	4	5
No time at all	Very little time	A little time	A moderate amount of time	A lot of time	A tremendous amount of time

5. **What person introduced you to gambling (identify the relationship)?**

   Father _____   Spouse or partner _____

   Mother _____   Friend _____

   Brother/Sister _____   Neighbour _____

   Aunt/Uncle _____   Work colleague _____

   Grandmother/Grandfather _____   Myself _____

   Other (specify) _____

6. **According to you, what triggered your gambling problem?**

   _____

   _____

   _____

7. **Currently, what are the main reasons why you gamble?**
   Let the person speak. Question him or her in order to identify one or the other categories. Make him or her choose one if he or she does not seem to have a preference.

	(check)	Indicate which ones
Do not gamble	_____	_____
To distract myself, think about something else, escape daily hassles	_____	_____
To make money or to resolve a financial problem	_____	_____
Other reasons	_____	_____

   Before asking this question, verify question 6 of the SOGS if the person thinks he or she has had a gambling problem over the last 12 months.

8. **Earlier, you mentioned that you think you have a gambling problem. How old were you when gambling became a problem for you**

   _____ years old

9. **On average, how much time do you spend gambling?**

   The information sought is very general. If the person says that he or she has recently decreased his or her gambling activities, refer to what he or she normally does.

   Per week? _____ (number of days)

   Per day? _____ (number of hours)

10. **On average, how much money do you spend gambling in one week (excluding wins)?**

   One week _____ $

11. **What is the total amount of money you have lost gambling until now?**

   Total losses _____ $

12. **Presently, to what extent does your gambling disrupt your social functioning (decrease in number of friends, isolation, giving up social activities, etc.)?**

   Read all the choices

0	1	2	3	4	5
Not at all	Very little	A little	Moderately	A lot	Tremendously

13. **Presently, to what extent does your gambling disrupt your professional functioning (less efficacious at work, absences, lateness, decreased concentration, etc.)?**

   Read all the choices

0	1	2	3	4	5
Not at all	Very little	A little	Moderately	A lot	Tremendously

14. **Presently, to what extent does your gambling disrupt your psychological functioning (mood, anxiety, depression, etc.)?**

   Read all the choices

0	1	2	3	4	5
Not at all	Very little	A little	Moderately	A lot	Tremendously

15. Over the past 12 months, have you SERIOUSLY thought about committing suicide (taking your life)?

    Yes _____   No _____

16. Was this thought mainly related to your gambling problems?

    Yes _____   No _____

17. (If "Yes") If you have SERIOUSLY thought about committing suicide over the past 12 months, have you determined how you would do it?

    Yes _____   No _____

18. Over the last 12 months, have you attempted suicide (tried to take your life)?

    Yes _____   No _____

19. Are you currently thinking about committing suicide?

    Yes _____   No _____

20. Just like gambling is a problem for you, are you currently experiencing problems in the following areas?

	Currently?	If not, have they already been a problem?	Comments (if any)
Cigarettes smoking?	_____	_____	_____
Drug consumption?	_____	_____	_____
Alcohol consumption?	_____	_____	_____
Consuming medications?	_____	_____	_____
Time spent on the Internet?	_____	_____	_____
Sexual behaviors?	_____	_____	_____
The frequency with which you purchase consumer goods (compulsive buying)?	_____	_____	_____
Is there anything else? (specify:)	_____	_____	_____

21. **Do you ever gamble under the influence of alcohol?**

        Yes _____   No _____

    If "Yes", for what proportion of the time?
    (For example, 1/10; reported in %)

22. **Do you ever gamble under the influence of drugs?**

        Yes _____   No _____

    If "Yes", for what proportion of the time?
    (For example, 1/10; reported in %)

23. **Could you tell me the financial consequences of your gambling?**

_____

_____

_____

24. **Have you ever declared a personal bankruptcy?**

        Yes _____   No _____

25. **Do you currently have any gambling debts?**

        Yes _____   No _____

26. **What is the amount of your gambling debts?** _____

Questionnaire based on the diagnostic criteria of the DSM-IV

Read each of the criteria as they are written here. After a first reading, if the person does not comprehend them very well, you could reformulate them so that they are well understood. For each of the 10 criteria of the DSM-IV, it should be very clear whether you can say Yes or No, to whether the person meets the criterion. If there is any doubt, ask more sub-questions. Certain gambling behaviors, such as increasing the bet (Q2) and the desire to chase losses (Q6), are typical of gambling problems. If the person responds No to these criteria, it would be important to double-check the answer.

1. **Are you ever preoccupied by gambling (for example, preoccupation with reliving past gambling experiences, planning the next gambling session, or thinking of ways of getting money with which to gamble)?**

    Yes _____   No _____

2. **Do you need to gamble with increasing amounts of money in order to achieve the desired excitement?**

    If the person does not understand:

    Do you have the tendency to increase your bets or do you always try to keep your bets at a minimum?

    Yes _____   No _____

3. **Have you ever made repeated but unsuccessful efforts to control, cut back, or stop gambling?**

    Yes _____   No _____

    3.1. What method(s), trick(s) or strategy(ies) did you use?

    _____

    _____

    _____

    _____

4. **Have you ever felt restless or irritable when attempting to cut down or stop gambling?**

Yes _____   No _____

Even if the person responded No to Q4, you must ask this question.

4.1. When you are gambling and it is impossible for you to continue gambling for various reasons (closing of the establishment, appointment, no more money, etc.), do you then feel restless, irritable or impatient?

Yes _____   No _____

4 2. **If "Yes"**, what is the intensity of this restless or irritability?

0	1	2	3	4	5
None at all	Very minor	Minor	Moderate	Severe	Very severe

5. **Do you gamble as a way of escaping from problems or of relieving a dysphoric mood (for example, feelings of helplessness, guilt, anxiety, depression)?**

Yes _____   No _____

6. **After losing money gambling, do you often return another day to get even (to "chase your losses")?**

Yes _____   No _____

7. **Do you ever lie to your family members, therapist, or others to conceal the extent of your involvement with gambling?**

Yes _____   No _____

8. **Have you ever committed illegal acts such as forgery, fraud, theft, or embezzlement to finance gambling?**

                    Yes _____   No _____

   8.1. **If "Yes"**, when was the last time? _____

   8.2. What illegal acts did you commit and how many times?

	Yes/No	Number of times
Forgery	_____	_____
Fraud	_____	_____
Theft	_____	_____
Embezzlement	_____	_____
Others (specify)	_____	_____

9. **Have you ever jeopardized or lost a significant relationship, job, or educational or career opportunities because of gambling?**

                    Yes _____   No _____

   9.1 **If "Yes"**, when was the last time? _____

   9.2. Which one(s)?   _____

      Family relationships   _____

      Spousal or partner relationships   _____

      Work relationships   _____

      Employment   _____

      Friendships   _____

      Studies   _____

10. **Do you rely on others to provide money to relieve yourself from desperate financial situations caused to gambling?**

                    Yes _____   No _____

   10.1. **If "Yes"**, when was the last time _____

Date of interview: _____ / _____ / _____

Clinician who conducted the interview: _____

Comments

_____

_____

_____

_____

_____

_____

_____

_____

_____

_____

_____

_____

_____

_____

_____

_____

_____

_____

INDEX

Index compiled by Liz Granger

CPSIA information can be obtained at www.ICGtesting.com
Printed in the USA
237811LV00002B/4/A